About the Author

Jonathan has been interested in travel and transport from a very early age. Firstly it was in the road network, bus and coach services. Later on his interest was oriented towards railways and trains. He then became interested in aviation and how it has developed. Jonathan has been fascinated with the way in which Heathrow Airport has developed in a piece meal way since the small aerodrome on a small part of the site for use during the 1914 to 1918 war.

Jonathan J.G. Lewin

LONDON HEATHROW AIRPORT
JUNE 2021

AUSTIN MACAULEY PUBLISHERS™

LONDON · CAMBRIDGE · NEW YORK · SHARJAH

A CIP catalogue record for this title is available from the British Library.

ISBN 9781528925969 (Paperback)
ISBN 9781528964517 (ePub e-book)

www.austinmacauley.com

First Published (2021)
Austin Macauley Publishers Ltd
25 Canada Square
Canary Wharf
London
E14 5LQ

Table of Contents

Diagrams

Introduction

When attempting to write about London Heathrow Airport, one must take three matters into consideration.

The foundations on which the airport was initially built remain unchanged, early planning decisions still define how the airport operates to this day.

The first consideration is that London Heathrow Airport has developed very much on what can best be described as a "piece meal" basis between when the idea of building an aerodrome on the site was first considered and to – day; unlike many other airports and their infrastructure around the world which were constructed "from scratch in one go". Every development and change was thought of as modem and as state of the art as and when it was completed, only for there to be subsequent developments and those which had previously taken place to be regarded as old fashioned, basic and out of date.

The second consideration is that aviation and in particular civil aviation and its developments over the years must also be taken into consideration.

The third consideration is that London had used different aerodromes for civil aviation in the past which have since been closed or are no longer used for Civil Aviation; and now has five airports for Civil Aviation of which only London Heathrow and one other is within Greater London.

I will therefore: first write about latter two of these considerations and then at the end of this thesis consider British Airways which has and is still regarded as the United Kingdom's national airline.

I will mention that as I am if fact interested in travel and transport generally. It will therefore look as if I am "going off at a tangent" in a number of places by writing about forms of transport other than aviation.

Preface I

Developments in Aviation in the United Kingdom

Aviation, in particular Civil Aviation, has developed on what can best be described as "a piece meal basis" within the United Kingdom.

At the same time, I will have to consider aviation throughout the world. The United Kingdom cannot be considered in isolation.

Until the end of the nineteenth century; all overland traffic was horse drawn (Other than the railways with steam locomotives from the middle of the nineteenth century); or over water by boat or ship (Whether horse drawn next to a towpath, sails, or rowing); methods of travel which were still significant in the 1930s.

The origins and early years of aviation must first be considered:-

1. The earliest of what in any form could be defined as aviation was the flying of kites in China in the fifth – century B.C. The flying of kites slowly spread around and over time became popular throughout the remainder of the world.

2. The world's first aerial voyage took place in France in November 1763, the first British balloon flight was in September 1784 and the first balloon flight across the English Channel was in January 1785.

3. The world's first power driven aircraft flight lasted for twelve minutes in the United States of America in on 17th December 1903 by the Wright brothers, the first power – driven aircraft within the Unites Kingdom was in October 1908 and the first power driven aircraft across the English Channel was in 1909.

4. The world's first aviation meeting took place in France in 1909, which aroused public interest in aviation, after which many governments realised that future military activity would also take place in the air and therefore formed air forces.

5. Small aerodromes were created around the United Kingdom subsequent to 1908; all of which were privately owned.

6. All aircrafts were privately owned.

7. The British Government formed the Royal Flying Corps on 13th May 1912 and the Royal Naval Air Service on 1st July 1914.

The First World War between August, 1914 and November, 1918 had a major impact on aviation. Many governments around the world including the United Kingdom took over all existing aerodromes and created further aerodromes for military use. The Air Force Act of 29th November, 1917 created the Air Ministry in the United Kingdom as it was realised that aviation required government control. The Royal Air Force was formed on 1st April, 1918 within the United Kingdom by the amalgamation of the Royal Flying Corps and the Royal Naval Air Service.

The First World War ended in November, 1918. Aerodromes around the world were turned over to private ownership throughout the World, except for the small number required for government or military activity. The British government passed the Air Navigation Act on 27th February, 1919 under which the Air Ministry became responsible for all matters relating to aviation, whether military or civilian, state or privately controlled; and could determine the conditions under which passengers, goods and mail could be conveyed by air to, from and within the United Kingdom. The British government determined that all British aerodromes would be open to civil aviation on 24th April, 1919.

It could be said that civilian air transport really started in 1919. The world's first scheduled international service took place on 25th August, 1919 with one passenger; which was between Hounslow Heath Aerodrome and Paris with a journey time of two hours fifteen minutes. The first airline meal (A luncheon) was introduced on 11th October 1919.

I will consider the general position between April, 1919 and April, 1922:-

1. Only the very wealthy were able to travel by aviation. They accepted the general Spartan basic conditions of flying as they regarded it as a special privilege. They were not concerned about facilities or comfort.
2. Terminal buildings were very basic (Or spartan). Passengers walked between terminal and aircraft even if wet and windy (Aircrafts were parked on the apron almost next to the tensional doors as there were fewer aircrafts). Luggage was taken by trolley between terminal and aircraft and arriving passengers collected their luggage from trolleys immediately outside of the terminal building.
3. Aerodromes were not used by more than sixty aircrafts a day anywhere.
4. Aircrafts were driven by propellers, were small and could only accommodate a small number of passengers (Never more than six passengers).

5. Pilots navigated by means of looking at landmarks, roads and the coast along their routes – Air Traffic Control (As now known) was non – existent.
6. Runways had about six inches of concrete.
7. Before each departure, a meteorological briefing was sent to the airline crew for the route of the flight, followed by telephone calls about the weather; and after each flight arrival, an observer collected a meteorological report on the weather for transmissions to other aircrafts in flight.

The only noticeable change in aviation between April, 1919 and the outbreak of World War Two in September, 1939 were:-
1. The introduction of air traffic control as a result of the 1922 Paris disaster. On 7th April, 1922, the pilot for an aircraft dropped below the clouds to be able to look for Landmarks, which resulted in a collision in which seven people died. It was therefore decided to introduce radar, radio stations and air traffic control to navigate aircrafts to and from airports. However, these air traffic controllers could only give red or green lights for take – off and acknowledge position reports as sent by radio.
2. By the 1930s, those people fortunate enough to be able to use aviation were expecting higher standards of comfort and on board facilities in line with their general financial statuses.

As a result of the outbreak of World War Two in September, 1939, civil aviation was suspended within many parts of the World. In the United Kingdom, the Air Navigation Order of 1939 was passed under which all civil aviation ceased; all aircrafts, airports and aerodromes were requisitioned by the Air Ministry; and were only available for military use.
The Second World War ended in May, 1945:-
1. On 10th May, 1945, wartime restrictions on Civil Aviation were revoked and the Civil Aviation Division of the Air Ministry became a separate Ministry known as the Ministry of Civil Aviation. This newly created Ministry of Civil Aviation directly controlled all civilian aviation air traffic control and all civilian aerodromes; while the Air Ministry only remained responsible for military aviation.
2. British based private and foreign airline operators (Both state and privately controlled) resumed operations within the United Kingdom in 1946 (nb there were no British based state controlled airlines until February, 1946).

Between 1945 and 1949, the Air Ministry handed many aerodromes over to the newly created Ministry of Civil Aviation. Airports remained very basic and by the standards of to – day very spartan (But a world war had only just finished and the "war time spirit" remained within the whole of society for some time afterwards) and aircrafts carried between six and thirteen passengers and meteorological offices for aviation were introduced in 1948.

The Air Ministry itself was absorbed into the Ministry of Defence in 1950.

In 1950, the manufacture, maintenance and operation of aircrafts were very costly, which meant that it was only accessible to the armed forces, the most senior government officials and the wealthiest (nb everyone else travelled by land and sea).

In 1951, all airlines only offered one (Unnamed) class of travel, within which all airlines were offering all of the facilities which at the time could be associated with top class passenger travel, taking into consideration the duration and distance of the flight. Subsequent to 1951, it was realised that as the cost of operating aviation fell, more and more people would travel and that it had become practical to provide a less expensive "class of travel" with more seats in each row and basic catering in the less preferred sections of the aircraft. Between 1951 and 1959, airlines operators around the World gradually introduced the less expensive Tourist Class accommodation on to sections of their airlines, which enabled people to travel who could not otherwise have afforded to do so. The accommodation which was not so changed became known as First Class. The increases in airlines and passengers over this period meant that more and more aircraft accommodation was converted from First to Tourist class.

The 1964 to 1972 period requires serious consideration:-

1. As the numbers of airline passengers was continuously increasing; it was realised that the existing propeller based aircrafts could not accommodate everyone; and that it would not be possible to park all aircrafts close to the terminal buildings.
2. Jet aircrafts were therefore used as they could accommodate eight times as many passengers and travel further then propeller based aircrafts – Larger aircrafts could accommodate 350 passengers.
3. Larger aircrafts needed more space to load and unload.
4. The technology of jet aircrafts enabled larger aircrafts which could accommodate more people, move faster and fly at higher altitudes. Propeller aircrafts were not as efficient as jet aircrafts as there was a limit to their possible sizes which reduced the numbers of passengers who could be carried on any one flight, they could not travel at as greater speeds and propellers required air which meant that they could not use the higher altitudes as could be used by jets where the air was thinner.
5. It was realised six inches of concrete was insufficient for runways – Concrete over two yards thick was therefore laid in steel cages – It had to be smooth and strong.
6. Runways had to be constantly monitored and kept clear of all objects as the smallest objects (e.g. Plastic cups, plastic bags and small cracks) could cause accidents; a very skilled task as it involved "removing needles from haystacks" while aircrafts were continuously landing and taking off.
7. Terrorists realised that aeroplanes made ideal targets – The searching of passengers became essential – The metal detector was used as hand searching was slow – More sophisticated systems were subsequently introduced as metal detectors could be outwitted, bombs could be assembled on aircrafts, the numbers of passengers were increasing and passengers were carrying more and a greater variety of shapes and sizes of bags.
8. Terminal buildings began to accommodate more shops and catering facilities as it was realised that passengers wanted more facilities while waiting; and that revenue could also be raised by letting out areas of terminals to shops and restaurants.

9. Many passengers who were reasonably affluent and or travelling on business travelled Tourist as opposed to First Class. More and more people could afford to fly and therefore made use of Tourist Class. This was still not a problem as the numbers of people who could afford to travel by aviation were still very limited. In "real" terms (As opposed to cash terms) the lowest 1971 fares between any two locations in the world was still sixteen times the lowest 2005 fare and still more than the 2005 price of a ticket in the most expensive class of travel .

The increase in passengers in the late 1960s and early 1970s had its effects:-
1. It was realised that it would not be possible to park all aircrafts close to the terminal buildings and that larger aircrafts would need more space to load and unload.
2. Walkways were constructed from terminal buildings to enable passengers to walk and disabled passengers to be taken to and from aircrafts without the need to go out of doors or to use stairs. "Travelators" helped to reduce the need to walk.
3. The increases in the amount of luggage passing through airports meant that it was no longer realistic for bags to be handled manually – Bar codes were introduced to direct luggage automatically in 1974, which meant that luggage could be moved around the airport automatically – As bags came in a wide variety of sizes and shapes, the mechanism had to be able to read the bar codes from a variety of directions – Also essential is a second bag system in case the main system breaks down – Facilities had to be provided to store the luggage of passengers who preferred to take their luggage to the airport and deposit it prior to their time of travel.

In January 1972 were structural changes to British civil aviation:-
1. The Ministry of Civil Aviation was absorbed into the Department of Transport.
2. Two public corporations were created
   2.1 The British Airports Authority to take over responsibility for all airports.
   2.2 The Civil Aviation Authority to take responsibility for air traffic control and telecommunications; aviation safety and standards generally; advising the government on civil aviation matters generally; and the licensing of engineers, aerodromes, aircrafts and members of flight crew.

It is a good idea to consider developments between 1972 and 1983:-

1. Terminal buildings became known as such between 1972 and 1974. Before then they were not known as terminal buildings, but by a variety of different {Appropriate) names or often simply as the aerodrome or airport buildings. I have only used the word "terminal" in previous paragraphs for simplicity.

2. Airline travel, whether domestic, European, or long haul all began to become affordable to ordinary people.

3. In 1978, the price of the least expensive domestic flight was still higher than the open first class rail ticket (Between locations with airports).

4. Low Cost (No frills) services started in 1978 but they remained very much "in their infancy" until after 1983.

5. "In House Entertainment" became available to first class long haul flights from 1972 and has been available to all passengers on all long haul flights since 1980.

6. Basically, there have been three types of market since 1980; passengers travelling on business, passengers visiting friends/relatives and people on holiday.

7. It was realised that the nature of airline passengers was changing in that greater numbers to people were travelling by air, airline operators could and were therefore competing to transport more passengers at lower fares and that airports were becoming more crowded with lengthier queues.

8. In 1978, smaller airline operators around the World began selling their tickets at the airports themselves on a stand by basis as opposed to selling their tickets in advance (e.g. Freddie Laker's Skytrain between Gatwick and the United States of America). The purchasing of tickets from airlines by people at airports themselves as and when travelling and accepting that they might have to queue for seats was less expensive than the traditional method of purchasing them in advance. As stand by passengers were causing congestion in terminals, this system was no longer permitted after 1980.

9. Walkways with travellators were constructed to allow direct access between terminals and aircrafts with boarding gates and enclosed waiting areas at each aircraft stand. Moving between terminal and aircraft became significantly easier. Walkways were initially bi directional with departing and arriving passengers only segregated within the terminal buildings themselves, but since the mid – 1980s new terminals and new extensions to existing terminals have had separate walkways for arriving and departing passengers, generally with one walkway above the other.

10. Prior to 1972, airline lounges in airports were not considered to be really necessary for anyone as fewer people were travelling by air and adequate facilities were available within the departure lounges themselves. (nb It was only the wealthiest who were able to travel by aircraft). Between 1972 and 1974, airline lounges in airports became available for first class passengers to allow privacy, as more and more people were travelling by air and departure lounges were becoming more crowded.

Tourist Class was re – named Economy Class on almost all airlines between 1980 and 1982. More and more people wanted to travel by airline whether on long or short haul flights, who would accept crowded terminals with lengthy queues and the minimum amount of comfort and attention on board, in order to travel as cheaply as possible. Only basic airline seating, accommodation and catering were provided.

Club Class (Often referred to as Business Class), the class between first and tourist class, was gradually introduced throughout the world in between 1978 and 1982 and in fact replaced first class on short haul flights:-

1. Many employers which would not allow their employees to use first class would allow them to use a new class of travel which was more expensive then Tourist Class.

2. Likewise, there were reasonably affluent people who were unwilling or could not afford to pay for first class, but who no longer wanted to use tourist class.

3. The majority of businessmen, wealthy people and other people who travelled frequently wanted a smooth efficient service with journeys no longer than necessary without crowds or lengthy queues at airports; as opposed to comfort or luxury.(nb The main concern for businessmen was to perform well while at their destination and then after they returned to their base).

4. Business class offered a separate faster check in, a higher luggage allowance, separate lounges prior to departure to provide an

appropriate environment apart from the general crowds, seating at the front of the aircraft, food/refreshments served on china crockery with silver cutlery and to be able to disembark with luggage unloaded before passengers travelling Economy Class.

Since 1978 many people, including businessmen and the wealthy, preferred "Low Cost No Frills" airlines as they preferred saving money to "frills and comforts".

First Class has permanently been retained for long haul flights as there were passengers who would pay higher fares to travel in luxury.

By 1985, it was possible for people in the United Kingdom to take a holiday more cheaply in the United States of America then elsewhere in the United Kingdom; and for people in Scotland or North West England to take holidays more cheaply in Spain more than in Ayr or Blackpool.

More and more Low Cost (No frills) services were introduced between 1985 and 1995; with numerous Low Cost domestic, European and long haul services.

The British Airports Authority was privatised in 1987.

By 1995, aviation had become available to virtually everyone in the United Kingdom, irrespective of their personal financial circumstances; long haul aircrafts could carry as many as 450 passengers; and here were domestic services between virtually every location with an airport in the United Kingdom with fares which were the same as coach services. In fact, one could travel to virtually any location in the world for the same price as an open standard class rail return ticket for longer journeys within the United Kingdom.

It must be noted that since the opening of the Channel Tunnel in 1995, many people have travelled between the London, Paris and Brussels regions by rail irrespective of financial position or reasons for travel.

It is a good idea to consider the average overall earnings in relation to fares. I will use the return London/Sydney route as the example. No figures are given in order to avoid confusion over inflation:-

1. 1950 – The lowest possible return fare was double average annual gross earnings.
2. 1955 – The lowest possible return fare was the same as average annual gross earnings.
3. 1959 – The lowest possible return fare was 65% of average annual gross earnings.
4. 1965 – The lowest possible return fare was 49% of average annual gross earnings.
5. 1980 – The lowest possible return fare was 12% of average annual earnings.

6. 1995 – The lowest possible return fare was 3% of average annual earnings.

I will consider terminals in the late twentieth and early twenty first century:-

1. It was realised that main buildings with one or more satellite buildings (Linked by dedicated underground rail) was the preferable design for terminals as the inconvenience of lengthy walkways was erased, aircrafts could be parked on three sides of the main building (With departure lounges on two levels) and all four sides of the satellite buildings.
2. Aircrafts remained in terminals for an average duration of ninety minutes (To include the unloading of passengers/luggage, refuelling, servicing and the loading of passengers/luggage), which meant that a quick turnaround is therefore essential.
3. Many terminals had around 1,200 aircraft movements a day.
4. Terminals had to be able to accommodate the Double Decker Airbus 380 (Which could carry over 700 passengers).
5. The Advance Passenger System was gradually being introduced whereby pods on the land side transport passengers between terminals, car parks and public transport.
6. In a number of instances, around 100 million passengers passed through airports annually and baggage systems had to handle 4,000 bags an hour.
7. Whereas bus and rail passengers could use alternative forms of transport; passengers travelling across water, across terrain over which rail or road were not really options, or distances in excess of 600 miles had no alternative to aviation.
8. Signposting and directions should be clear in the same font – Pictogram's should only be used for easily imaged facilities like taxis and telephones.
9. Shops on the airside were meant to serve the passengers and not vice versa.

10. The appearance of terminal buildings was considered to be important. "In" were space, daylight and views; "Out" were corridors and enclosed spaces. Affluent passengers and businessmen who travelled on very short flights with only one class of travel (i.e. Economy Class) and had paid the highest fares, expected to be treated in the same manner as passengers who were travelling club/business class on longer flights – It has therefore been policy since 2000 for passengers paying premium fares on flights only offering one class to be allowed to use the check in and lounge facilities as available to people travelling club/business class on longer flights.

Towards the very end of the twentieth century, it was realised that there were passengers who or their employers were prepared/able to pay for a standard of travel higher than ordinary Economy Class but not Business/Club or First. A new class known as Premium Economy Class was therefore created on most long haul flights; within which passengers were offered slightly larger seating in the aircraft, either in the generally preferred areas in the main cabin or in a separate cabin next to the main cabin, but otherwise everything remained identical to normal Economy Class.

Subsequent to 2010, the British Airports Authority was separated into separate enterprises for each airport.

In 1949, airlines moved at a maximum speed of 230 miles an hour and only had a range of 2,000 miles; by December 1960, they had a maximum speed of 300 miles an hour and had a maximum range of 4,300 miles; and since 1982 have had a maximum speed of 600 miles an hour with a maxim range of 6,500 miles.

In 1949 any form of aviation was only for the wealthiest of people. Since 1985 most people have taken flying half way round the world or further for granted.

As far as the future (i.e. Post 2018) is concerned, one remains impossible predict with accurate certainty as to what will happen regarding passenger aviation. Numerous predictions and experiments have taken place around the world, which have either not taken place or been subsequently dropped for financial reasons or for reasons of practicality. Different predictions are still being made but no one can say whether or not they will be take place or would be viable.

FLIGHT DURATIONS and NUMBER OF INTERIM CALLS
IN 1953, 1965 and 1985

Virtually no change since 1985
Blank means no direct flights at the time, changing required.

Amsterdam	------------	------------	1hr 35min (0)
Belfast	2hr 8min (0)	1hr 15min (0)	1hr 15min (0)
Edinburgh	2hr 3min (0)	1hr 20min (0)	1hr 20min (0)
Glasgow	2hr 16min (0)	1hr 20min (0)	1hr 20min (0)
Inverness	------------	------------	1hr 40min (0)
Newcastle	------------	1hr 30min (0)	1hr 5min (0)
Amsterdam	2hr 30min (0)	1hr 10min (0)	1hr 10min (0)
Athens	7hr 30min (1)	3hr 45min (0)	3hr 40min (0)
Brussels	1hr 50min (0)	50 minutes (0)	50 minutes (0)
Copenhagen	2hr 35min (0)	1hr 35min (0)	1hr 30min (0)
Dublin	------------	1hr 15min (0)	1hr 15min (0)
Lisbon	4hr 45min (0)	2hr 25min (0)	2hr 25min (0)
Madrid	4hr 30min (0)	2hr 40min (0)	2hr 40min (0)
Paris	1hr 35min (0)	55 minutes (0)	55 minutes (0)
Rome	3hr 40min (0)	2hr 5min (0)	2hr 5min (0)
Stockholm	4hr 35min (1)	2hr 10min (0)	2hr 10min (0)
Vienna	5hr 10min (1)	2 hours (0)	2 hours (0)
Cairo	7 hours (1)	4hr 35min (0)	4hr 35min (0)
Delhi	17hr 40min (4)	14hr 5min (4)	9hr 5min (0)
Johannesburg	21hr 30min (5)	14hr 30min (2)	10hr 15min (0)
Los Angeles	------------	------------	10hr 20min (0)
New York	17hr 15min (0)	7hr 35 min (0)	7hr 5min (0)
San Francisco	------------	15hr 50min (1)	10hr 10min (0)
Singapore	25hr 30min (6)	20hr 15min (4)	12hr 30min (0)
Sydney	84hr 30min (7)*	30hr 10min (6)	23hr 15min (1)
Tokyo	36hr 20min (8)	25hr 10min (5)	11hr 10 min (0)
Toronto	------------	7hr 40min (0)	7hr 30min (0)

*London/Sydney involved two overnight stops in 1953

nb Between 1953 and 1965, sea crossings between Liverpool/Southampton and New York generally took five days (Four days and ten hours as an absolute minimum)

Preface II
Airports and Aerodromes in the London Area

There have been aerodromes in the London area since before the First World War. During the First World War, all existing aerodromes were taken over by the government and further aerodromes were constructed for military purposes.

When the First World War ended in November 1918, aerodromes were turned over to private ownership throughout the World, except for the small number required for government or military activity. However some of these aerodromes were not used and were allowed to become derelict land.

Between the two world wars, the aerodrome near Croydon and what has since become known as R.A.F. Northolt were London's two airports for passenger civil aviation. The aerodrome near Croydon was improved and extended and came into operation as the new Airport for London on 30th January 1928 (Officially opened on 2nd May, 1928).

Upon the outbreak of war in 1939, all airports and aerodromes were once again taken over by the government for military purposes.

During the Second World War, the government increased the size of what would become London Heathrow Airport as it needed a larger airbase then it then had and considered the land terrain in that area more appropriate for such an airbase.

After the Second World War in 1945 the government decided that Heathrow Airport would be London's main passenger airport as it was surplus to military requirements and passenger aviation was likely to expand and to use Northolt for military purposes. The airport near Croydon was permanently closed and the airport at Northolt was permanently transferred to the Royal Air Force in 1959. The airports at Croydon and Northolt were considerably smaller then at Heathrow. However, Northolt continued to be used as an overspill for London Heathrow until April, 1974.

London currently has five airports for passenger civil aviation purposes, of which only two London Heathrow and London City are within Greater London. All of these have developed on a "piece meal" basis except for London City Airport.

I will now consider each of these airports in greater detail.

The aerodrome which has become London Heathrow Airport was constructed for military purposes during the First World War, it became derelict after the war, it was developed as a private aerodrome in 1929, taken over by the government for military purposes and expanded to its present size during the Second World War and since the end of the war has been London's principal passenger airport. It has services to/from virtually every location in the world and patronised by virtually every nationality in the world.

II (a) London Gatwick Airport

Gatwick Airport is owned by the Global Infrastructure Partners.

Gatwick Airport is located in West Sussex within the Borough of Crawley, between Horley in Surrey and Crawley in West Sussex, half way between London and Brighton. It is twenty nine and a half miles south of central London, the same north of Brighton and three miles north of Crawley. The railway station is next to the south terminal on the London/Brighton railway. The airport is located immediately to the west of the A23 London/Brighton road and there is a road link to the M23.

There are local bus services to and from Crawley, East Grinstead, Hawley, Horsham, Reigate and Redhill. There has been an hourly coach service between Gatwick and Heathrow airports since May 1967.

The airport has a single runway and two terminals (The North Terminal and the South Terminal). The South Terminal, which was opened on 27th May, 1958, is linked to the railway station* line by an undercover walkway. The North Terminal, which was opened on 18th March 1988, is linked to the South Terminal and the railway station* by a monorail or automatic passenger mover (* Served by all train services between London and the Sussex coast).

I will now consider the history of the airport:-

1. The name Gatwick dates back to 1241 when there was a manor of that name on the site. The manor remained until the nineteenth century.
2. A racecourse was created beside the London/Brighton railway in 1891 and there was a station, known as Tinsley Green, which included sidings for horse boxes.

3. From the late 1920s land adjacent to the racecourse was used as a private aerodrome. It initially belonged to the Surrey Aero Club, which from August 1930 used a former farmhouse as its clubhouse. From 1932, ownership frequently changed hands. It was licensed for non – private flights in 1934 and there was some commercial aviation from June 1935. A new railway station opened in June, 1935, with the route between the station and the aerodrome under cover. The aerodrome was closed between 6th July, 1935 and 6th June, 1936 for a terminal (As would now be known) to be built.
4. The aerodrome was put under military control between September 1939 and 1945.
5. The terminal was in constant use for charter flights from June, 1935 until it became obsolete in the 1950s (Except between 1939 and 1945 when it was requisitioned for military purposes). The airport was prone to fog and water logging; and two fatal accidents in 1936 had cast doubt on its safety.
6. The government decided that Gatwick would be the alternative airport to London Heathrow in 1950, such development started in 1952, it was closed between 1956 and 27th May 1958 for renovation and it was opened by the Queen on 9th June, 1958.
7. The re – opening in 1958 included an under – cover walkway between the terminal and the railway; and was the first British airport with piers, air bridges, and walkways between terminal building and aircraft. Since then it has been used for all types of airlines and flights.
8. What had been a local railway station known as Tinsley Green was enlarged and was re – opened as Gatwick Airport Station on 27th May 1958.
9. The airport doubled in size and the runway was extended in 1962.
10. As a result of changes in local authority boundaries on 6th May 1974 the area covered by the aerodrome was transferred from Surrey to Sussex.
11. The Gatwick Express was introduced in 1984.
12. The North Terminal opened on 18th March 1988, after which the South Terminal (The only terminal until then) was given substantial refurbishment.
13. The Brook House immigration removal centre was opened by the Home Secretary on 18th March 2009.
14. Ownership was transferred from the British Airports authority to the Global Infrastructure Partners on 3rd December, 2009.

II (B) London City Airport

London City Airport is in the London Borough of Newham just under seven miles to the east of the City of London. It is used mainly by domestic and European flights but also by a few long haul flights. It is owned by a consortium consisting of several companies.

The airport was first proposed in 1981 as a part of the docklands development by the then Chief Executive of the London Docklands Development Corporation and it was opened on 31st May 1987 for short haul and domestic flights.

The airport has been served by the Docklands Light Railway since the 2nd December, 2005. Consideration was given to allowing access to Crossrail (To open later 2018 and over 2019) either by the re – opening of Silvertown station (A scheme supported by the London Borough of Newham) or a walkway to/from Custom House Station but nether were considered to be practical for various reasons.

The airport has long since been seen as a hub for business travellers due to its proximity to the City, but the numbers of leisure travellers have been increasing due to congestion at other airports. It was used by half a million passengers in 1995, long haul flights with only Club Class have been using the airport since 29th September 2009 and by 2012 twelve airlines with twenty nine destinations were using the airport

Ownership of the airport transferred from the British Airports Authority to a consortium of companies on 30th November 2005.

Ii(C) London Luton Airport

Luton Airport is in the Borough of Luton thirty five miles north of Central London and one and a half miles to the east of the centre of Luton. Flights.

The airport is used mainly for low cost "no frills" domestic and European

Transport links include a road between the airport and the M1; and a railway station on the main London/Luton! Bedford/Leicester/Sheffield line to the south of Luton itself with a dedicated coach service between the airport and that station.

Flying commenced to and from the aerodrome in 1937, buildings for use for administrations and terminals (As now known) were planned and the aerodrome was officially opened on 16th July 1938.

The aerodrome was used for military purposes during World War Two and afterwards was transferred back over to civil aviation. Subsequent to 1946, many airline companies started and subsequently without warning stopped using the airport and tenninals (As now known) were frequently replaced. The government encouraged charter companies to use this aerodrome from 1951.

The present runway was opened in 1959.

Between 1959 and 1972, the availability package holidays on airlines to and from this airport enabled many people to take holidays abroad. 20% of all foreign holidays were to and from this airport in 1971.

Plans for it to become one of London's main passenger airports were put forward in 1979 and approval was given in 1986. It was on 11th July 1987 that the present terminal was opened and that the airport became recognised as an international airport. It was renamed London Luton Airport in 1990.

Public transport access opened in 1990 were:-

1. The railway station to the south of Luton and the dedicated coach link to and from this station were opened in 1990. Until then passengers travelling to and from the airport by rail had to use local bus between the airport and the centre of Luton.

2. A road link between the M1 and the airport via the A6 and the railway station to the south on Luton.

Since 1990, the airport has been used mainly for low cost "no frills" domestic and European flights; and its passengers have either come from a radius of thirty miles or from the south midlands generally.

The airport is at present owned by Luton Borough Council.

II (D) Stanstead Airport

Stanstead Airport is in the district on Uttlesford in the county of Essex, thirty miles north east of Central London and three miles east of the village of Stanstead Mountfitchet.

The airport is used mainly for low cost "no frills" domestic and European flights.

The airport has one main terminal, with three passenger satellite buildings where all passenger gates are.

The airport has a dedicated railway and station, the railway links into the London Liverpool Street/Cambridge/Ely/Kings Lynn line and there is a road link between the London/Cambridge M11 (Where it crosses the A120) and the airport.

The aerodrome was built in 1943 and continued to be used by the Royal Air Force until 1949; when it was transferred over to civilian use, handed over to the Ministry of Civil Aviation and was used for charter airlines.

However, there were very few passenger services in the 1950s and 1960s.

It had been intended that this would be London's third passenger airport since 1964, but a decision to use this airport was not confirmed until 1984 due to strong local opposition. Between 1964 and 1984, alternative sites were considered, but none were considered practical for a variety of reasons (e.g. Too expensive, would involve destroying more properties, the nature of the soil, would interfere with wildlife, or access by ordinary passengers might be difficult).

Formal approval for its development was given by the government in June 1985 and construction work was completed in March 1991.

Since March 1991, it has been used mainly for low cost "no frills" and some charter domestic and European flights.

Opened in March 1991 were:-

1. The railway link to and from the London/Cambridge/Ely/Kings Lynn line. (Until then one had to use London/Cambridge railway to as far as Stanstead Mountfitchet or Bishops Stortford and then travel by local roads to/from the airport.
2. The road link to and from the London/Cambridge M11 where it met the A120 (Prior to then, one had to use local roads between the Mll/A120 junction and the airport). The Mll had been in place since 1977; prior to when one had to use local roads between the airport and the All and then the All which passed through all local towns and villages between London and Norwich via Epping, Bishops Stortford, Stanstead Mountfitchet, Newmarket and Thetford) and did not have any dual carriageways.

The airport is at present owned by Stanstead Airport Plc.

Plans to Use All Five of London's Airports Equally.

In the mid – 1990s it was suggested that all five airports could be used equally to prevent overcrowding at Heathrow; but this was rejected for two main reasons.

Many passengers were in transit and transporting passengers between airports could become complicated. Air Side buses would have had to have used the ordinary Land Side roads between airports, with the risk of passengers who were intent on avoiding passport/customs controls escaping from these buses when held up at road junctions or in traffic queues.

Although people in the United Kingdom have been familiar with all five airports, foreigners travelling to London might not be as familiar and might not understand that the five airports are in different locations within South East England.

Chapter I
Some Basic Features of London
Heathrow Airport

London Heathrow Airport is now known as Heathrow Airport Plc and is currently (i.e. 2018) owned by Heathrow Airport Holdings.

As with all other airports within the United Kingdom, the airport holds a Civil Aviation Authority Public Use Aerodrome License which allows flights for flying instruction and for public transportation of passengers.

The airports co-ordinates are 51.28 degrees north and 0.27 degrees west, and its elevation is eighty three feet (twenty five metres).

London Heathrow Airport as such has developed on what can best be described as a piece meal basis since the First World War.

The area of the site of the airport is 3,002 acres (12.14 square kilometres). It is currently (i.e. 2018) located in the London Borough of Hillingdon around fourteen miles (twenty two kilometres) due west of Charing Cross/Trafalgar Square. Round the airport are Windsor (west), the M25 (west), Colnbrook (north west), Longford (north west), Harmondsworth (north), Hayes (north east), Hounslow (east), Hatton Cross (east), Feltham (south), Stanwell (south west), and Staines (south west).

London Heathrow Airport currently (i.e. 2018) is the largest and busiest airport in the United Kingdom, the busiest airport within the European Union, and the third busiest airport in the world in terms of passenger traffic. It handles more international traffic than any other airport in the world.

A number of rivers flow within close proximity of the airport:-

1. The Thames runs in a half circle to the south; through Richmond which is 4.35 miles due east from the most easterly part of the airport; near to Walton which is 5.25 miles due south from the most southerly point of airport; through Staines which is 2.75 miles south west and the nearest point of the river to the airport; and near to Wraysbury which is 3.25 miles due west of the most westerly part of the airport. Had the Thames run in a direct line between Westminster and Windsor (or any of its locations further west), it would have run into the north of the airport.

2. Two rivers run in a north/south direction, both with their mouths at the River Thames; the River Colne, two fifths of a mile to the west at the most westerly part of the airport which joins the Thames near Staines; and the River Crane, one fifth of a mile to the east of the most easterly part of the airport which joins the Thames opposite Kew Gardens.

3. The Duke of Northumberland River and the Longford River, both leave the River Colne north west of the airport, run in a south easterly direction within close proximity of each other, and pass either side of Longford. The Duke of Northumberland River flows into the River Crane near to Feltham, and the Longford River to the River Thames close to Hampton Court. They were rerouted twice, firstly when the Government expanded the aerodrome during the Second World War, and again when Terminal Five was constructed between 2000 and 2008 to remain outside of the perimeter road – they had passed either side of the Perry Oaks Sludge Disposal Sewerage Works both inside the perimeter road until Terminal Five was constructed.

The airport is bordered by the A4 (London/Reading/Bristol road), the A312 (Kingston upon Thames/Harrow Road), the A30 (A4 at Hounslow, Staines, South West England road), and the Stanwell Moor Road (Staines/Longford road).

The Perry Oaks Sludge Disposal Sewerage Works were constructed on a site to the west of the village of Perry Oaks in the early 1930's to the north west of where the aerodrome would be constructed. It was named after the neighbouring small village. When the aerodrome was expanded during the Second World War, the village itself had to be demolished; but the sewerage works remained fully intact and fully operational immediately inside the aerodrome's perimeter road until the construction of Terminal Five between 2000 and 2008 when they were relocated to Iver South in Buckinghamshire.

The airport has two main runways both running in an east/west directions as in 2018. Such capacity has not been increased since 1946.

Terminals have been opened at different times since 1946. Terminal Five opened to passengers on 27th March 2008. Terminal Two was demolished and rebuilt between 2009 and 2014. Terminal One is in the process of being demolished and rebuilt as in 2018.

A number of statistics need to be considered:-
1. On 1st January 1946, only five passengers passed through and only a handful of staff were employed within the airport.
2. Throughout 1946 alone; 63,151 passengers and 2,386 tons of cargo passed through the airport while there were around 2,046 aircraft movements.
3. By 1951, a total of 796,000 passengers has passed through the airport since 1st January 1946 – most people used luxury liners as they were still cheaper than the cheapest airline ticket.
4. By 1952, a total of 860,760 passengers has passed through the airport with 52,000 flight movements since 1st January 1946.
5. By December 1953, a total of 1,200,000 passengers and 23,000 tons of cargo had passed through the airport with 62,000 flight movements since 1st January 1946.
6. Three million passengers passed through the airport in 1956, four million in 1959, and five million in 1960.
7. A total of 6,100,00 passengers passed through the airport (41,600,000 in total since January 1946) and 136,000 tons of cargo in 1962; with as many as one million passengers in any one calendar month.
8. 12 million passengers and 276,000 tons of cargo passed through the airport in 1966.
9. Fifteen million passengers passed through the airport in 1969.
10. Twenty seven million passengers passed through the airport in 1980.
11. In 1986, thirty one million passengers and 537,130 tons of cargo passed through the airport with 315,755 aviation movements (i.e. landings and departures).
12. Forty million passengers passed through the airport in 1990.
13. In 2000AD, sixty five million passengers and 1.3 million tons of cargo passed through the airport with 466,800 aviation movements (i.e. landings and departures).

It is a good idea to consider the position in 2006:-
1. By 2006, fourteen million flights and 1.4 billion passengers has passed through the airport since 1st January 1946.
2. Around 50,000 people were employed within the airport.
3. Ninety airline operators from eighty five countries fly to 210 destinations.
4. Sixty eight million passengers, seventy five million items of baggage and 1,200,000 tons of cargo passed through the airport a year. (nb 210,000 passengers, 1,300 flights, and 50,000 vehicles arrive or depart daily)
5. Twenty four million ornamental fish, 300,000 chickens, 150 reptiles, 23,000 birds, 1,200 horse, 12,000 cats/dogs and 19,000 other animals passed through the airport.
6. Fifteen hotels around the airport offered over 5,700 rooms.
7. The coach and bus station were the busiest in the United Kingdom with over 1,600 services daily both to and from over 1,000 locations.
8. 11% of all passengers are domestic, 43% short haul, and 46% long haul.

Of the airports sixty nine million passengers in 2011, 7% were bound for British destinations, 41% were short haul international travellers, and 52% were long haul international travellers. The busiest single destination in terms of passenger numbers was New York with 3,800,000 passengers.

In 2013, sixty eight million passengers used the airport, which was used by over ninety airlines which flew to over 170 destinations worldwide.

I will now consider the position as in 2017:-
1. The airport was occupied to 99.2% capacity.
2. There were 480,000 aviation movements (i.e. flights landing and leaving the airport); around 1,400 aviation movements daily (one every forty five seconds).
3. Seventy eight million passengers passed through the airport (which did once reach 236,000 in one day); of which 64% began or ended in the United Kingdom.
4. 1,541,000 tons of cargo passed through the airport
5. Over 90 airline operators used the airport with 185 destinations in over 90 countries.
6. 80% of all long haul flights to and from the United Kingdom used London Heathrow Airport

7. 93% of all flights were international and 7% domestic. Of the 93% international flights, 40% were to/from elsewhere in Europe, and 25% North America.
8. 30% of all passengers were on business, and 70% leisure.
9. It was the largest port of entry for overseas visitors.
10. 34% of all passengers were making connections.
11. 48% of all aircraft movements were by British Airways.
12. The airport has 123 stands served by airbridges, seventy remote stands, and twelve cargo stands.
13. The airport was at the heart of an international transportation crossroads.
14. The 170,000 employees (to include directly employed full time staff, employees of outside concerns like shops, and contractors) bring a great sense of comradery and purpose with a fixation on safety, and a spirit rare in modern culture.
15. Against a backdrop of significant constraints, the airport operates successfully.

Ensuring a safe and efficient operation is a complex task requiring compliance with established international rules.

The fuel farm, fire station, and new control tower are all located between Terminal Five and the Central Area. There is an additional fire station on the north west corner of the airport.

Daily arrivals and departures start and 4.30am and 6.00am respectively.

As the prevailing wind was from the west based on historical wind directions, it was decided in the 1950's only to use the two east/west runways for landing and taking off, with all others used as taxiways.

Hotels are located along the A4 near to the Central Area Access Road, near to Terminal Four, and near to Terminal Five.

The International Royal Mail Sorting Office at the airport opened in 1984 and is located next to the cargo terminal on the south westerly side of the airport (before which International Mail was dealt with at the Mount Pleasant Sorting Office in Central London).

Other buildings include the administrative buildings (whether airport, aviation, airline, government, or otherwise) and aircraft hangars are in the main area located near to Hatton Cross on the south eastern side of the airport.

Policing the airport is the responsibility of the aviation security of the Metropolitan Police, although the armed forces have occasionally been deployed at the airport during periods of heightened security.

Full body scanners are now in use at the airport. Passengers who object to their use after being selected can opt for a full manual search in a private room, and those who still object are not allowed to fly.

The airport sustains 76,000 jobs directly and also 116,000 indirectly in the immediate area.

General maintenance has to take place overnight.

The airport has Anglican, Catholic, free church, Hindu, Muslim, Jewish, and Sikh chaplains. There are prayer rooms and counselling rooms in each terminal. The respective chaplains organise and lead prayers at certain times in the prayer rooms.

Grass on the airfield is always kept at twenty centimetres high to prevent birds from settling, as birds are unable to spot predators at this height.

It is worthwhile noting a piece of information. King George VI and the Queen (as she was at the time) travelled to the airport to see their daughter (Princess Elizabeth as she was at the time) with her husband Prince Philip, Duke of Edinburgh depart on a five month tour of the Commonwealth on 31st January 1952. At 4.06pm on 7th February 1952, H.M. Queen Elizabeth II (as she had become) returned as her father had died. This meant that the airport was the first location on British Soil which she touched as the Queen. There is a plaque on the Renaissance Hotel at the exact location where the Queen stepped onto the ground. (nb Hotels were subsequently built over and around the areas of the airport where passengers boarded and disembarked aircrafts prior to 1955)

DIAGRAM I
The Central Area as in 2018

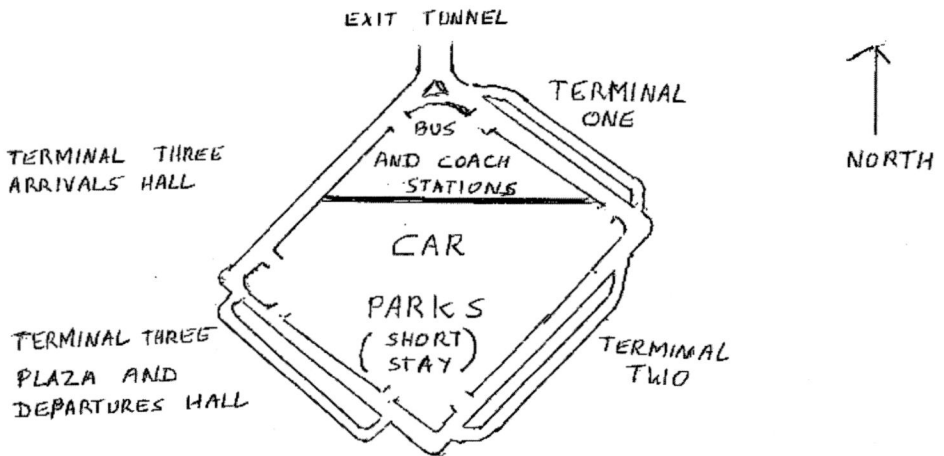

EXIT TUNNEL

TERMINAL ONE

NORTH

BUS AND COACH STATIONS

TERMINAL THREE ARRIVALS HALL

CAR PARKS (SHORT STAY)

TERMINAL THREE PLAZA AND DEPARTURES HALL

TERMINAL TWO

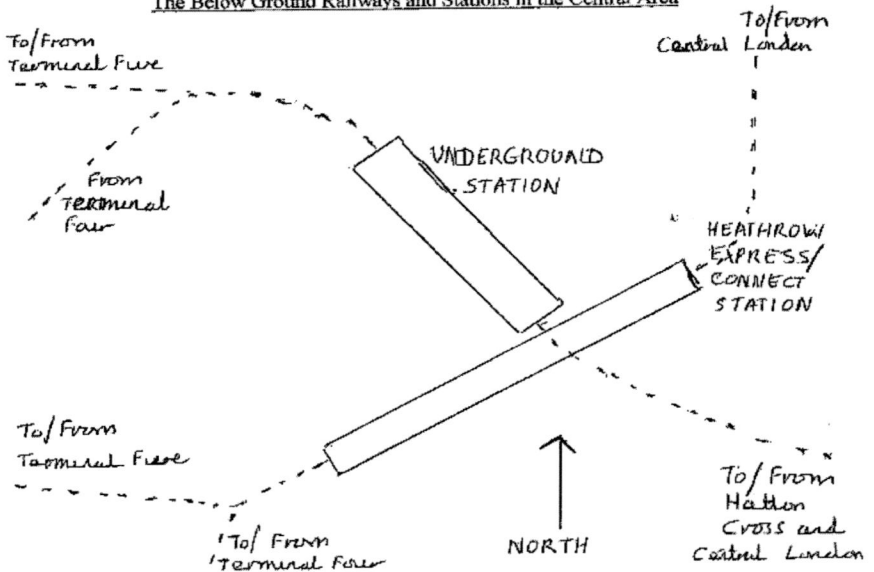

The Below Ground Railways and Stations in the Central Area

To/From Terminal Five

To/From Central London

From Terminal Four

UNDERGROUND STATION

HEATHROW EXPRESS/ CONNECT STATION

To/From Terminal Five

To/From Terminal Four

NORTH

To/From Hatton Cross and Central London

DIAGRAM II
The Airport as in 2018

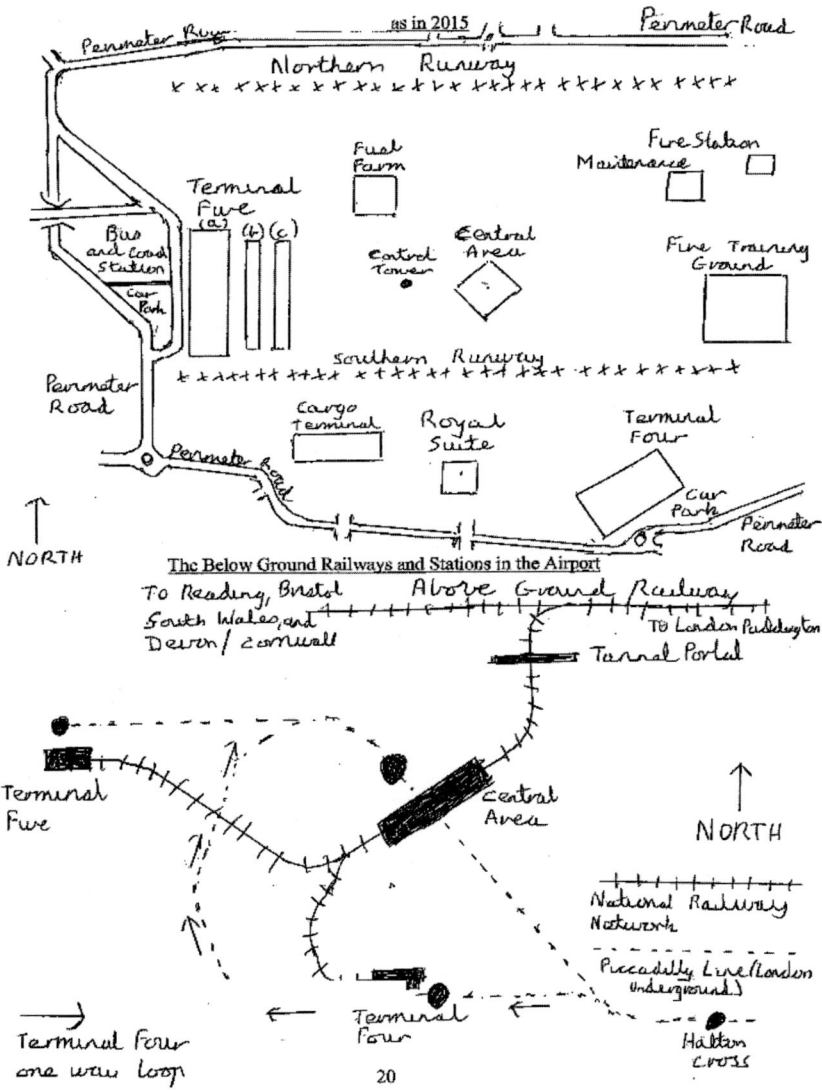

Perimeter Rnp.   as in 2015   Perimeter Road

Northern   Runway

Fuel   Fire Station
Farm   Maintenance   □

Terminal
Five
(a) (b) (c)   Central
                            Area
        Central   Fire Training
        Tower   Ground

Bus
and Coach
Station

Car
Park

Southern   Runway

Perimeter
Road

Cargo   Royal   Terminal
Terminal   Suite   Four

Perimeter Road   Car
                                                  Park
                                                        Perimeter
                                                        Road

NORTH

The Below Ground Railways and Stations in the Airport

To Reading, Bristol   Above Ground Railway
South Wales, and
Devon / Cornwall   To London Paddington

                                        Tunnel Portal

Terminal
Five   Central
                                Area   NORTH

                                        National Railway
                                        Network

                                        Piccadilly Line (London
                                        Underground)

Terminal Four
one way loop   Terminal   Halton
                    Four   Cross

DIAGRAM III
The Area Surrounding the Airport as in 2018

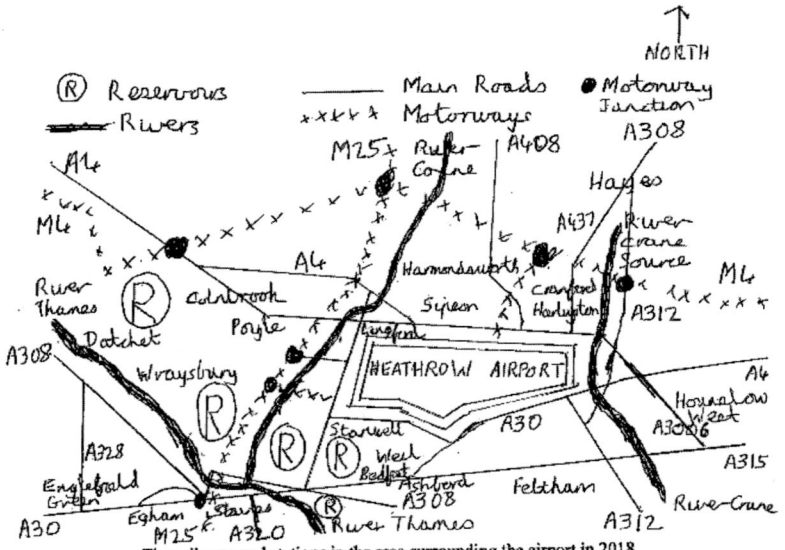

The railways and stations in the area surrounding the airport in 2018

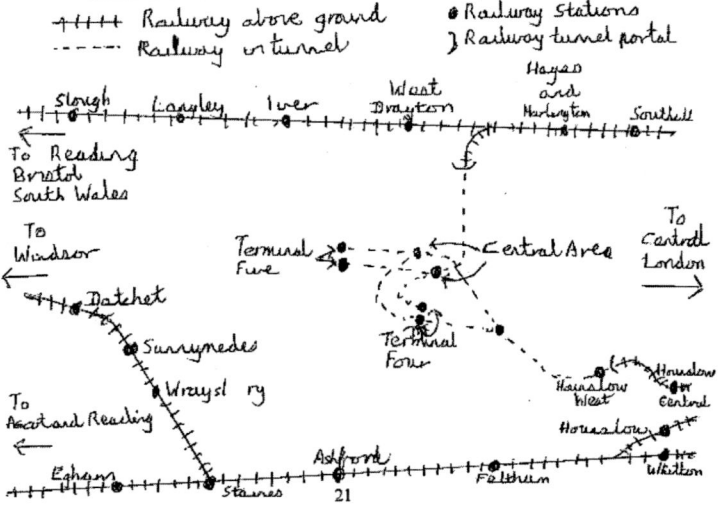

Chapter 2
The History of London Heathrow Airport

London Heathrow Airport has developed very much on what can best be can best be described as a "piece meal" basis since the construction of the first aerodrome on the site during the First World War. Every development as it happened has been regarded as the most modern in aviation, only to be superseded by a subsequent development which made the makes the earlier one out of date.

2.1 The Location of the Airport Prior to Any Aerodrome or Aviation on the Site

The land was and is a series of flat gravel terraces roughly twenty – five to 100 feet above sea level, based in the Thames Valley with soil of overlay gravel; and therefore well drained and therefore suitable for the construction of an aerodrome.

The site occupies the south west corner of the former Hannondsworth parish with the Bath Road (The main road between London and Bath prior to 1925) forming a convenient boundary between it and the remainder of the parish. The extreme south east was a part of Hounslow Heath. It was within the then County of Middlesex.

Heath Row was a pre Roman settlement which became a hamlet in what was an agricultural area with good agricultural land; with the land around mostly farmland, market gardens and orchards. It consisted of an isolated row of cottages and a fann along a small country road. It became known as Heath Row, a name which can be traced back to as far back as 1410, as it was on the north west edge of Hounslow Heath. It was bordered on the west by open fields. The hamlet was roughly where Terminal Three now is and the farm roughly where Terminal One is.

Perry Oaks was a village with a fann located in the then county of Middlesex immediately to the south of Longford, east of the Longford River and west of the Duke of Northumberland River. To the immediate west of the village was Tithe Barn Lane, which roughly followed a north/south route.

There were and are two rivers, the Duke of Northumberland River and the Longford River. They both left and still leave the River Colne to the north west of the aerodrome site and both ran in a southerly direction on either side of the village of Longford. They then passed either side of the Perry Oaks village and farm, with the Duke of Northumberland River to the east and the Longford River to the west. They both then ran in a south easterly direction easterly direction. The Duke of Northumberland ran and still runs to the north of Feltham and joins the River Crane near Baber Bridge. The Longford River ran and still runs through Feltham to join the Thames near Hampton Court. The Duke of Northumberland River formed a boundary between Stanwell and Hannondsworth.

I will now consider the area covered by the site in general:-
1. There were a number of remote and rural villages forming a part of the larger parish of Hannondsworth – There was wildlife and the area was popular for picnics and families.
2. The parish of Hatton was the most northerly part of the Parish of East Bedford to the south.
3. Tithe Bam Lane was on the west side of the former village and farm of Perry Oaks.
4. The villages to the north of the Bath Road (i.e. The main road between London and Bath prior to 1925) pre date that road.
5. The area was surrounded by a number of old villages – Colnbrook, Cranford, East Bedford, Harlington, Harmondsworth, Longford, Poyle, Sipson (North of the M4 and east of the M4 spur road), Stanwell and West Bedfont; all rich in history.
6. There were fruit growing orchards.
7. Bath Road (The London/Bath road until 1925) lies between two geological formations.

The roads in and around the site included:-

1. The road between London and Bath took its current route from the City of London as far as Knightsbridge; the present A315 along the southerly border of Hyde Park, past the Royal Albert Hall on the northerly side and then Olympia on the southerly side and then through the centres of Hammersmith and Chiswick; then along the present Heath: field Terrace and Wellesley Road to the northerly side of Kew Bridge on the River Thames; then along the present A315 through Brentford, Isleworth and Hounslow; then along the A3006 past Hounslow Barracks (Now Hounslow West) station on the northerly side; then along the current route of the A4 past the airport (As it would become in 1944) on the southerly side; then through the villages of Longford, Poyle and Colnbrook; then along the current route of the A4 thereafter.

2. The road between Hounslow and the south west of England took the route of the present A315 between the centre of Hounslow and where the A315 meets the current route of the A30; then along the current route of the A30 to as far as the present Staines by pass; then through the centres of Staines and Egham; and then along the current route of the A30 for almost the whole of the way to Cornwall.

3. The road between Harrow and Kingston via Hayes followed the current route of the A312 except between the current A315 and Hayes; it followed Faggs Road to as far as Hatton, then along a direct route to the junction between the A4 and the current A437 and then along the current route of the A437 through Harlington to Hayes.

4. Tithe Bam Lane between Bath Road and the post 1925 A30, passed Perry Oaks Village and Farm on the westerly side and then through Stanwell.

5. The post 1925 route of the present day A30 Great West Road was a local road between the A4 and where Terminal Four now is. The local road then left the current route of the A30 to pass through West Bedfont to join Tithe Bam Lane in Stanwell. Most people still travelled on horseback or horse drawn vehicles in 1910, though there was a limited amount of motorised transport.

The only railways anywhere near the site were:-

1. The Great Western Railway Company's railway between London and the west country, with local stations at Hayes and Harlington, West Drayton and over as the nearest stations. All trains were hauled by steam locomotives.

2. The Southern Railway Company's railway between London and Reading with stations at Feltham and Ashford. All trains were hauled by steam locomotives as line was not electrified until 1930.

3. The Metropolitan and District Railway Company's railway terminus at Hounslow Barracks (Currently Hounslow West Station on the Piccadilly Line) one mile to the west of the centre of Hounslow, which had been electrified between 1903 and 1905.

DIAGRAM IV

The Area Covered by the Airport Site as in 1912

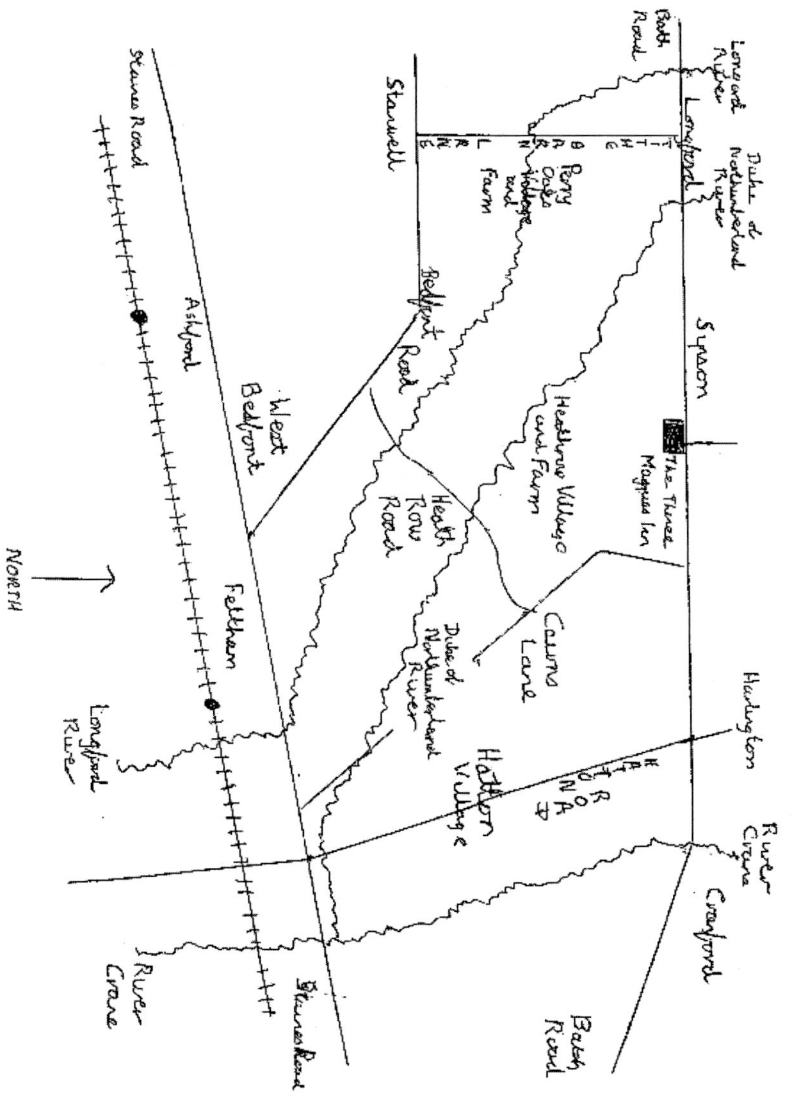

Surrounds of the Area Covered by the Airport Site as in 1912

2.2 .The First Aerodrome on the Site

An aerodrome was first constructed on the site in 1915; but like a number of aerodromes in the London area and the remainder of the country was constructed for military purposes during the First World War and became disused after the "military aviation rundown" when the war ended in November, 1918. It was a lot smaller at 748 acres than the airport now is. The site was chosen for the building of an aerodrome; as the land was basically a flat deposit of gravel; without trees, railways, or other obstructions; it was within close proximity of a number of rivers including the Thames which meant there were numerous places for water to flow during heavy rain; and just high enough above the water to avoid flooding; which basically made the land ideal for aviation. It had a single runway. It was bordered on the south by a local road (Which between 1925 and 1930 was developed as the A30 main road to Staines and the South West of England), the Duke of Northumberland River to the south west, High Trees Lane to the west, the hamlet and farm of Heath Row to the north west, Cains Lane to the North East and the pre 1944 route of the road between Harrow, Hayes and Kingston upon Thames to the east.

2.3 The Period Between 1919 and the Outbreak of the Second World War

The site was disused between 1919 and 1929.

Road numbering was introduced throughout the country and through routes were re–routed in South East England between 1925 and 1930; the A4 and A30 became respective through routes and the A406 was made into a through road known as the North Circular Road. Many of the roads of the current through routes did exist before then, but as through routes and there were no flyovers or by passes. (nb Some parts of the pre 1925 route of the London/Bath road still bear the name, Bath Road)

In 1929, aviation engineer and aircraft builder Richard Fairey purchased a 150 – acre site from Harmondsworth Parish Church between the A4 and A30 to the south east of the then Heath Row village and fann, where the ground was level; initially to develop for flight testing aircrafts designed and manufactured at his factory in North Hyde Road nearby. After test pilots tested aircrafts on the site, it was recommended for development as an aerodrome for ordinary use. It was opened for private aircrafts in 1930, initially known as Harmondsworth Aerodrome and subsequently the Great West Aerodrome. (nb The public aerodromes were at Croydon and what has since become known as R.A.F. Northolt). In June 1936, the Middlesex County Council (As it was then known) rejected plans to extend the size of the aerodrome. Over this period of time, the aerodrome led a primitive existence as aviation was only for the wealthy few. Richard Fairey could not foresee how aviation would develop.

In the area on the site:-

1. Were fruit growing orchards, but these declined rapidly subsequent to 1919 due to the haphazard nature of the orchards and foreign competition.

    In the 1930s, ploughman's matches were organised by the Agricultural and Growers Association annually immediately after the harvest. The last was on 28th September, 1937. The 1938 match was cancelled because of the prolonged drought. (nb The 1939 to 1944 matches were cancelled because of the war and they were not resumed after the war as all' suitable sites had been buried in concrete).

    The West Middlesex Drainage Scheme as inaugurated in the early 1930s involved a large sewerage works at Mogden in Isleworth, the sludge disposal works at Perry Oaks and seventy miles of new pipes. Two million people were served within an area of 160 square miles, The main works in Mogden were in the middle of a populated area which would not tolerate a sludge works as a neighbour. The sludge was therefore pumped from Mogden to the disposal works to the west of Perry Oaks Village on the other (Westerly) side of Tithe Barn Lane; what was then a remote area some seven miles away from the main works at Mogden, where the settling lagoons would cause less of a problem. The site for the sludge works was chosen as it was then isolated from existing dwelling houses (Separated from Perry Oaks village and farm by Tithe Barn Lane), building development in the immediate vicinity was then considered unlikely, the land was low cost and it was three miles from the nearest train station. The site of the sludge disposal works occupied 250 acres of land. The pipe from Mogden followed the route of the Bath Road and then the then Tithe Barn Lane. Entry to the sludge disposal works was then originally on the easterly side from Tithe Barn Lane (The village and farm were east of this lane). Had the pipe taken a more direct route the construction of the airport to its present size would probably have been very difficult.

2.4 The Second World War 1939 to 1945

All aerodromes were taken over by the government and were only available for military use under the provisions of the Civil Aviation Order of 1939.

Development of the airport in 1945 to its present size started in 1944 for military purposes. A site was required for an aerodrome to and from which aircrafts could land and take off in any weather. Other airfields were considered but not considered appropriate due to trees, hills, soils and more properties to demolish. The site was chosen in preference to others because of the nature of the soil, the flatness of the land, its proximity to water (i.e. The various rivers) and fewer trees to remove or properties to demolish.

It was felt that the sacrifice of the land was justified as there were no suitable areas of land for aerodromes in the London area with lower agricultural potential, the area was flat without hills, the nature of the soil, there were places for water to run during heavy rain, fewer properties were destroyed then on other sites and only 15% of good agricultural land in the area was destroyed.

The Air ministry requisitioned the surrounding houses, orchards, farms and roads in April, 1944 and construction work began in May, 1944. The hamlet known as Heath Row, the village of Perry Oaks and their adjoining farms were demolished. The A312 had to be re – routed to its present day route to bypass the airport to the east and the Longford and Duke of Northumberland rivers were re – routed to their 1944 to 2003 routes to the west and south of the extended runways. Public houses, farms, most of the village of Hatton and parts of Hartington and Harmondsworth to the south of Bath Road (To include the villages of Heath Row and Perry Oaks) were demolished in 1944.

The Perry Oaks Sewerage Works were not demolished as this was opposed by the Middlesex County Council since there was nowhere else to re – locate them.

Excess water was channelled into the River Crane to the east and the River Colne to the west of the aerodrome; as well as the Longford and Duke of Northumberland Rivers. Several reservoirs were constructed to hold water "overflows" from the rivers; to include two on either side of the re – routed A312 (Next to the River Crane to the south east of the aerodrome); and three to the west the Staines (i.e. The King George VI, the Wraysbury and the Queen Elizabeth Reservoirs the latter of which was renamed The Queen Mother Reservoir in 1955).

There became six runways in three pairs in the shape of a hexagram, in order that aircrafts could land and take off in any direction, with at least two runways always within thirty degrees of the wind direction (Given the prevailing wind, only two remain in operation to this day, though the others are used as taxi ways). An R.A.F. control tower was also constructed.

The extension of the airfield to its current size was still under construction when hostilities ceased in May 1945. (nb There was no guarantee that the war would end in 1945).

It must be noted that the construction of the airport would not have been possible and would have been rejected by a public enquiry in peace time due to local objections. The outbreak of war gave the Air Ministry the opportunity to purchase land compulsorily.

Tithe Barn Lane was closed, replaced by the Stanwell Moor Road on the westerly side of the Perry Oaks Sludge Disposal Sewerage Works.

2.5 The Period from 1945 to December 1955

The end of the Second World War in May 1945 requires consideration:-

1. The Government created a separate Government Department, the Ministry of Civil Aviation and handed many aerodromes including the one at Heathrow over to this new Department.
2. On 23rd May, 1945, the Government decided that:-
   2.1 Heathrow would be used as London's main passenger airport instead of Croydon or Northolt as it was envisaged that passenger aviation was likely to increase and the newly completed runways would otherwise have become redundant.
   2.2 Northolt as the military aerodrome as that aerodrome was considered to be appropriate for military operations when there was no war.
3. Alternatives to using Heathrow as the main passenger airport had been considered; but it was concluded that none of these alternatives were practical for different reasons (e.g. Trees, hills, the nature of the soil, existing buildings, the ability to expand to accommodate future demand). Potential sites included:-
   3.1 Sites in Essex, Hertfordshire, Kent, North East London.
   3.2 A number of locations near the airport including Denham, Hanworth, Heston, Hounslow, Northolt and a combined sea and airport in Woolwich;
4. However, Northolt continued to be used as an overspill for Heathrow Airport's passenger civil aviation activities until April 1976 when all of Heathrow's activities could be accommodated within the airport itself.

The next period to consider is between 1946 when the airport became London's principal passenger airport and December, 1955 when the central area was first opened:-

1. RA.F. occupancy officially ended on 25th January, 1946.
2. The airport was opened on 18 January, 1946, a cold foggy day; but except for one flight there were no flights for a further eighteen days. The official opening took place on 31st May, 1946.

    2.1 The passenger and cargo buildings used were located next to each other along the southerly side of the A4 London/Reading/Bath/Bristol Great West Road to the east of the post 1955 easterly access road (i.e. The tunnel between the A4 Great West Road and the post 1955 central area) near where the Renaissance Hotel is now located as in 2017.

    2.2 The control tower, which was next to the passenger buildings, had been constructed by the Royal Air Force.

    2.3 Passengers, though wealthy, accepted the general facilities though spartan, primitive and basic by to – days standards, as the blitz spirits and attitudes adopted as a result of the Second World War were still prevailing and they regarded flying as a special privilege.

3   The initial buildings, which more resembled an army outpost were made of canvas and very primitive (i.e. E military marquees).

    3.1 The waiting room was a marquee with tea/coffee served at one end, comfortable chairs, small tables and vases of flowers.

    3.2 There were also telephone boxes, a pillar box and a mobile post office.

    3.3 There was another marquee with a W.H. Smith and Son.

    3.4 Times of departure chalked on a giant notice board next to airline flap, staff also called across the marquee to call passengers to assemble.

    3.5 In hot summer weather, the flaps were opened to allow in fresh air; but there was no heating which meant it was cold and damp in winter, also the marquee often leaked when it rained.

    3.6 The toilets were primitive.

    3.7 Wooden duckboards were laid between the marquee and the aircrafts in order that passengers did not sink in the mud.

    3.8 Royal Air Force mobile caravans were used as staff offices.

4   The marquees and caravans were replaced by prefabricated buildings (With the same materials used as for building prefabricated homes) towards the beginning of 1947 in the same location as the tents and marquees.

4.1 Although still basic and spartan by the standards of to – day, they were a distinct improvement.

4.2 These prefabricated buildings were larger, more spacious, warmer and were more comfortable then the tents with proper lighting.

4.3 Passengers still walked between the prefabricated buildings and aircrafts even if the weather was wet and windy (nb Aircrafts could always be parked on the apron almost next to the apron side doors of the prefabricated buildings on the apron side as there were not as many aircrafts).

4.4 Times of departure were still chalked on a giant notice board next to the airline flap, staff also called across the departure areas to call passengers to assemble.

5   In the post 1947 prefabricated building, the same area was used for checking in, passengers awaiting departures and people awaiting arrivals.

5.1 The check in desks for departing passengers, where passengers handed in their luggage and collected their boarding passes, were on the apron side of the building).

5.2 Departing passengers produced their boarding passes as they walked from the building on to the apron once their flights had been called and passed through passport control as they boarded the aircraft (As they left the building during wet or very cold weather).

5.3 Arriving passengers had their passports checked by immigration officers as they disembarked from the aircraft (Inside the aircraft during wet or very cold weather), collected their luggage from trolleys outside of the customs hall and then passed through customs.

5.4 Within the building were a bar, a cafeteria, a post office and telephones.

5.5 Luggage was taken by trolley between the building and aircrafts and arriving passengers collected their luggage from trolleys immediately outside of the building before passing through passport and customs controls.

6   There was also a public observatory.

7 Subsequent to 1946, consideration was given to expanding the airport north of the A4 Bath Road (Great West Road) and south of what has since become the A30 Great South West Road; which would have involved the demolition of a number of a number of built up areas and uprooted several local communities; but these were permanently cancelled on 19th December, 1953 as a result of substantial local opposition.

8 By December, 1953, passenger traffic had reached one million with a total of 62,000 flights over the year.

A perimeter road was constructed around the whole airport in order that no one travelling within the airport had to use outside public roads. That has been except for the area around the 1946 to 1955 passenger and cargo buildings where there was a break in the perimeter road and one had to use the A4 Bath/Great West Road.

As more and more people were flying, passenger buildings and the aprons outside had to accommodate more and more passengers. Improvements to the facilities as had been available were considered essential as the airport and the buildings used by passengers were the first buildings which visitors to the United Kingdom first saw. Several schemes had been considered abroad at different times, all of which had potential problems. Construction of the central area began in 1950.

2.6 The Period from December, 1955 to September, 1971

Architect Sir Frederick Gibberd was appointed to design permanent buildings to cope with the rising numbers of passengers. His plan saw the creation of the central area in the middle of the airport between the parallel runways accessed by a tunnel under the northern runway to and from the perimeter road.

The tunnel was constructed by cut and cover due to the nature of the subsoil; which did involve the temporary closure of the northern runway.

The central area of London Heathrow Airport was officially opened by H.M. Queen Elizabeth II for passenger transport on 16th December 1955:-

1. The 158 acre Central Area housed:-

1.1 Two buildings the Europa Building and the Britannic Building (As Terminals One and Two were then known).

1.2 Administrative buildings known as the Queen's Building (Which housed offices).

1.3 The 122 foot high air traffic control tower.

1.4 .A bus station, car park (Able to accommodate 1,150 cars and twenty coaches).

1.5 The two passenger buildings were linked by bridges.

2 The smaller Europa building was located on the north east side and the larger Britannic building on the south east side; with the apron located immediately to the north east, east and north east of these two buildings. .In this way aircrafts could be parked close to the buildings, so as not to obstruct others arriving or departing:-

2.1 Aircrafts could be parked anywhere on the apron.

2.2 There was a passenger walkway inside the two passenger buildings immediately next to the apron for passengers to walk to and from the nearest gate to their aircraft; running continuously through both passenger buildings through the Queen's Building.

3 There were thirty four gates, each of which were divided in two. Coaches conveyed passengers to and from aircrafts.

4 There was a public observatory on the roofs of the Queens Building, access to which was through this building. There was a restaurant within the observatory.

5 Road access to/from the Central area was by means of a half mile tunnel to/from the perimeter road on the north side. It had a dual carriageway, separate cycle tracks, separate pedestrian pathways and could handle 2,000 vehicles an hour.

6 There were no plans for rail or underground services as it was not then envisioned that there would be sufficient demand for these facilities.

7 The only car parking facilities were in the car park Central Area itself as it was not then envisioned that demand for car parking would exceed availability.

8 For the first time, the arrival and departure areas were on separate levels in each of the buildings; and passengers waited for their departures in the departure lounges after passing through passport control – Passengers either walked or were bussed between buildings and aircrafts; depending upon distance between the buildings and the aircraft (There were no walk on/off facilities between airlines and buildings).

9 There were no facilities for domestic travel. Domestic passengers either used the 1947/55 terminal or R. A. F. Northolt. This meant that the 1947 to 1955 passenger building and R.A.F. Northolt continued to be used as an "overspill" for all domestic flights (– Together with some short haul international flights).

10 These new passenger buildings (Unlike the former prefabricated buildings) were modem, spacious, comfortable with smart check in facilities and numerous amenities (i.e. Restaurants, cocktail bars, lounges, hair dressing saloons, post offices, shops and car hire facilities).

11 There were no Victorian frontages to conceal the terminals, offices, control tower and car park – The theme was brick, stone and glass.

12 At the time, it was not realised that airline travel would increase and that further passenger buildings would be required in the future. The infrastructure was intended to make way for improved facilities, but not for growth in passengers.

Hangars for aircrafts and maintenance buildings were constructed to the east of the central area.

On 1st August, 1957, Sir Eric Melbourne recommended in his report the expansion of Gatwick Airport and that all London Heathrow passenger buildings (As terminals were then known) should remain in the Central Area with one central heating system for the entire airport.

In 1958, a new cargo building was opened on the south side of the airport south of the southern runway and the 1947 cargo building was penitently closed. It was connected to the Central Area by a tunnel, which became known as the Heathrow Cargo Tunnel in January, 1972.

The Oceanic Building (As Terminal Three was then known) facing south west in the Central Area was opened on 13th November, 1961 to handle long haul flights. At that time it only consisted of what has since become the departure side. After Gatwick Airport in 1958 it was the second terminal in the country to use piers, walkways and air bridges. Due to lack of space, British Overseas Airways Corporation and some others remained in the Britannic Building (As Tenninals Two was then known).

A number of hotels were located along the A4 between 1959 and 1961 where it ran parallel to the Perimeter Road at the northerly side of the airport.

The M4 between London and Maidenhead was opened in 1964; running about a mile to the north of the A4 at the airport. A new road giving direct access between the perimeter road and this motorway (And local roads immediately to the north of the motorway) was completed in 1965.

An interdenominational chapel was first proposed in 1965. The St Georges Chapel next to the control tower was dedicated on 11 October 1968.

By May 1968, the airport was handling fourteen million passengers annually.

2.7 The Period from October 1971 to June 1980

Security procedures were penitently tightened at the end of 1971 due to the Irish Republican Anny's (I.R.A.) mainland bombing campaign. Departing passengers had to pass through security controls to pass from the check in hall to the departure lounge. The public observatory was closed.

As with all other airports, ownership and control was transferred to the newly created British Airports Authority public corporation, the same time as the Civil Aviation Authority was created and the Ministry of Civil Aviation itself (i.e. What was left under direct government control) was absorbed into the Department of Transport.

The arrivals hall of the Oceanic Building (Terminal three) facing north east was opened early in 1972 and all long haul flights were transferred to this building:-

1. The departure and arrival areas were both at ground level, unlike the other two buildings where the arrival and departure areas on different levels.
2. The departure area faced south west and the arrival area faced North West.
3. There was a direct indoor link between the check in area in the departure building and the arrival hall.
4. There was a continuous linked walkway along the apron side of both buildings, with several "sprigs" along which were the departure gates.
5. The numbers of piers and air bridges were increased significantly

In 1972, the Britannic buildings continued to be used for short haul international flights; while R.A.F. Northolt and the former 1946 to 1955 buildings continued to be used by all domestic and a few short haul international flights.

Between April, 1972 and April, 1976, the smaller Europa building (Terminal One) was demolished and re – built:-

1. During this time all long haul flights used the Oceanic Building (Terminal Three); but more short haul international flights were transferred back to R.A.F. Northolt and the former 1947 to 1955 buildings.
2. The new building was opened to passenger aviation in April, 1976, it had moving walkways between the buildings and aircrafts, piers and air bridges and it had facilities for both domestic and international flights.

3. Domestic flights had a separate check in area, separate departure lounge, separate walkway and separate arrivals hall; as passport and customs control were not required.

The three terminals in the central area became known as terminals with their respective numbering from April 1974; but not the 1947 to 1955 buildings.

Prior to January 1972, there were six runways, running in pairs at different angles in the shape of a hexagon; but these were then reduced to the two east/west runways for landing and taking off as these were the only ones long enough to accommodate the landings and take offs of the newer larger aircrafts; with all others used as taxiways These two runways were extended from 9,000 to 12,000 feet. As aircrafts made more noise taking of then landing, policy was for aircrafts to take off and land in a westwards direction from east to west to minimise noise over London, unless the wind was such that landings and take offs had to be from west to east.

As more and more people were using the airport, more and more airlines were requiring areas for airline lounges and separate check in areas for passengers travelling first class. Airlines therefore began providing airline lounges and separate check in facilities within the airport for passengers travelling first class.

In April, 1976:-
1. R.A.F. Northolt was permanently closed to civil aviation and the 1946/55 passenger building was permanently closed, as the Central Area could then accommodate all flights. Immediately before closure, R.A.F. Northolt was taking on 10% of the airport's movements.
2. The passenger and cargo buildings became known as terminals, as with most airports around the world since early 1974. The new passenger terminal in place of the Europa Building became known as Terminal One, the Britannic Building as Terminal Two, the Oceanic Building as Terminal Three and the cargo building as the Cargo Terminal.

Walkways between the terminal building and aircraft stands and air bridges, were built on to Terminal Two between 1976 and 1978.

The Piccadilly Line extension construction commenced in April 1972, the extension to the central area was opened as far as Hatton Cross on 19th July 1975 and was fully opened on 16th December1977.

At the same time as the opening of the Piccadilly Line extension on 16th December 1977, underground walkways linking all three terminals, the underground station and the coach/bus station were opened.

2.8 The Period Since June, 1980

Since The Middle of 1980:-

1. It has been policy to reserve car parks near terminals for "short stay parking". Long stay car parks near the perimeter road on the northerly side were opened, with regular complimentary shuttle bus services to/from the terminals.
2. The British Airports Authority has been expanding the proportion of terminal space allocated to shops and catering establishments and has been routing passengers through these retail areas to maximise their exposure to retail offerings.
3. Passengers also wanted more facilities to be available while they were waiting in departure lounges.
4. There have been complimentary bus services between all terminals and local hotels.

As airlines gradually introduced business class between 1978 and 1982, the airport had to provide airline lounges and separate check in facilities for passengers using that class. Business class became popular as the airport became more crowded as there were passengers who did not want to or were unable to pay the first class fare, but wanted a smooth efficient service with journeys no longer than necessary without crowds or lengthy queues at airports; as opposed to comfort or luxury.

It has also been realised that there are many people who were not flying but who were use the airport (Central Areas) as an interchange:-

1. Between rail, tube, coach and bus services.
2. Passengers travelling between local areas to the north and west of the airport and Central London use local bus services between the local areas and the airport and tube (And rail since June 1998) between the airport and Central London.
3. Passengers making use of coach services to/from different parts of the country often found it more convenient to travel by rail (Since June, 1998), tube or local bus to/from the coach station at the airport then the Victoria Coach Station (Provided that the coach service on hand serves the airport).

4. People with points of origin or final destinations in Central London might use the railway/underground services between Central London and the airport and be collected or dropped off by car for local or long distance journeys if the airport is a more convenient place for collecting/dropping off then Central London.

By the early 1980s annual passenger numbers had increased to thirty million and required more terminal space. As a result, Terminal Four was constructed to the south of the airport to the east of the cargo terminal and was opened on 1st April 1986. It had direct access to the A30 and Perimeter Road. Like Terminals One and Two, the departure area was on the level above the arrival area. The waiting areas at the departure gates themselves were on what can best be described as an "open plan" basis. The walkways for departing and arriving passengers were on separate levels.

The British Airports Authority was privatised on 17th July, 1987.

When Terminal Four opened in April 1986, it was decided that all terminals would be used for both short and long haul flights, as opposed to having one terminal dedicated to long haul flights. Whereas arrivals and departures for short haul flights have been at continuous levels throughout the day, arrivals and departures for long haul flights have been in "peaks and troughs" (i.e. Very quiet at certain times of the day, but many flights to and from different locations around the world arriving and/or departing at virtually the same time of day).

The M25, which runs to the west of the airport, was completed in 1986.

The eastern extension of Terminal One (i.e. A further walkway in the international section with piers and air bridges) was opened in 1995. As with the then procedure, there were separate levels for arriving and departing passengers.

The Heathrow Express began providing a railway service between the airport and London Paddington on 23rd June, 1998 by means of a special railway line between the airport and the London/Reading/Bristol/South Wales main line.

The subject of Terminal Five requires detailed consideration.

1. The planning process was very lengthy. Consideration had to be given to the general environment, potential pollution, blight, access to/from the terminal and access between this and the other terminals. The possibility of a fifth terminal emerged in 1982 (Four years before the opening of Terminal Four). Planning studies commenced in February 1988, the proposal for this terminal was formally announced on 15th May 1992 and formal planning application was submitted on 17th February 1993. The public enquiry began 16th May 1995 and ended 17th March 1999 after sitting for 525 days. Government gave planning permission on 20th November 2001.

2. Construction began in September 2002 and the terminal was opened to passengers on 27th March 2008.

3. British Airways transferred its entire Domestic, most of its international and some of its Gatwick operations to this terminal when it opened as it had sole use.

4. As opposed to walkways, it had boarding gates on three sides of the main building and two satellite buildings each with boarding gates on all four sides.

5. It was located at the westerly end of the airport with direct access to/from the perimeter road, the Stanwell Moor Road (Between the A4 near Longford and the A30 near Staines) and the M25.

6. It became necessary to build a new taller air traffic control tower as the existing one did not have "communication" access to this terminal. As the airport had to remain fully open at all times, the tower had to be constructed off the premises and then taken to its location on three trailers and erected its location overnight (The five hours when the airport is closed). It entered service on 21st April, 2007.

7. The two rivers (The Duke of Northumberland River and the Longford River) had to be diverted immediately to the outside of the perimeter road and the Perry Oaks Sludge Disposal Sewerage Works (On the westerly side of the airport within the perimeter) had to be relocated to Iver South in Buckinghamshire in order not to pass under the terminal or its access areas

8. There are top grade hotels next to this Terminal.

Following the departure of British Airways from Terminal One in 2008, the terminal was re – designed in order to join the international and domestic departure lounges into one single departure lounge with both security controls available to all passengers using this terminal.

Terminal Three was refurbished between 2006 and 2007 to include a pedestrianised plaza complete with canopy in front of the building and new levels built above the existing walkways to accommodate arriving passengers (To enable complete segregation between arriving and departing passengers).

Terminal Four was refurbished between June, 2008 and 2010.

It was decided that Terminal Two and the Queens Building should be demolished and that a completely new terminal build on the site:-

1. Neither building had been refurbished since they were opened in December 1955, except for to build on the bidirectional walkways between 1974 and 1976.
2. Terminal Two was closed on 23rd November 2009.
3. The Queens Building was demolished in 2009 and Terminal Two during the summer of 2010.
4. Construction of the new terminal building began in November 2010 and it is was re – opened on 4th June 2014. Like Terminal Five, it had a main building and two satellite buildings.

Upon the breakup of the British Airports Authority in 2012, the company which took ownership of this airport Heathrow Airport Holdings became known as Heathrow Airport Pic.

The 1955 to 2008 control tower was demolished during the first part of 2013 to make way for new roads to link with the new Terminal Two.

Terminal One was closed on 29th June, 2015, is being demolished and re – built and is due to re – open between 2019 and 2021.

2.9 An Interesting Piece of Information

For anyone who is interested in travel and transport, the various methods and the history thereon, it is worth mentioning that there has always been a public house known as The Magpie on the southern side the London/Reading/Bath Bristol/Great West Road (The A4 since road numbering was implemented) immediately to the east of what has since become the access road between the M4 and the Central Areas (Terminals One, Two and Three). When the horse was the principal mode of travel (Whether horseback or horse drawn vehicles), the public house was a popular place to break journeys, take refreshments, give horses a break, allow horses to drink water and when desired to change horses.

Chapter 3
Aviation Operations and Regulations Applied to the Airport

It is a good idea to consider the aviation operations and regulations as applied to London Heathrow Airport.

As with all other airports within the United Kingdom, the airport holds a Civil Aviation Authority Public Use Aerodrome Licence which allows flights for flying instruction and for public transportation of passengers.

Pilots must re – train each move on a simulator if they have not undertaken to move concerned within twenty eight days. Landing and take offs are therefore always undertaken manually to keep pilots qualified for these manoeuvres.

Automatic pilot systems are useful while the aircraft remains in the air between locations, but landings and take offs are always undertaken manually:-

1. Automatic systems can fail.
2. Landings and take offs are delicate procedures which have to be undertaken delicately, accurately and carefully.
3. Speed and direction of the wind must be considered. When there are cross winds at the landing and take – off stage, the pilot must be able to keep the aircraft steady.
4. Pilots must re – train each manoeuvre on a simulator which they have not undertaken within twenty eight days.

Although a captain is in overall command of a flight, operations are a team effort involving not only flight crew but also cabin crew.

Landings and take offs generally always made against the wind as the wind makes take taking off easier and when landing helps to slow the aircraft down. When there are cross winds at the landing and take – off stage (Due to the layout of the runway), the pilot must be able to keep the aircraft steady

The two main runways generally operate in segregated mode, with one for arriving aircraft and the other for departing aircraft; though there are exceptional circumstances when this is not possible. These now operate at 98% capacity.

3.1 Air Traffic Control

The purpose of Air Traffic Control is to control the numbers of aircrafts in any particular air space; and to maintain minimum distances and heights between aircrafts.

Aircrafts change air traffic controllers as they change air space, which means that the controllers of different parts of the United Kingdom and the rest of the world must co – ordinate.

The air traffic controllers are responsible for permitting airspace to all users, making efficient use of airspace. This is complex as it involves more than two million flights carrying over 220 million passengers a year throughout the United Kingdom. Controllers keep landing aircrafts safely separated by allocating different heights to aircrafts and minimum horizontal distances.

Air traffic controllers are responsible for co – ordinating all aircraft movements within their air space, keeping aircrafts at safe distances from each other, assisting in preventing collisions between aircrafts and obstacles on airport aprons and runways, directing pilots around bad weather and ensuring that inbound and outbound traffic flows smoothly with minimal delays. Many airports have spare capacity and can therefore able to catch up on delays, but London Heathrow does not have that luxury (i.e. One small delay can have a drastic "domino effect" across the entire airport).

Flights in their initial and final stages are controlled at the airports themselves. Military controllers act as a backup and ensure that there is co – ordination.

Air traffic controllers at the Heathrow Approach Control (Based in Swanwick, Hampshire) then guide aircrafts to their final approach, merging aircrafts from the four holds into a single stream of traffic, sometimes as close as 2.5 nautical miles (2.9 miles, 4.6 kilometres) apart. Considerable use is made of continuous descent approach techniques to minimise the environmental effects of incoming traffic. Once an aircraft is established on its final approach, control is handed over to the Heathrow Tower.

As in 2017, air traffic control at London Heathrow Airport is complex as there are five terminals, 480,000 flights a year with seventy eight million passengers and 1,541,000 tons of cargo and must co – ordinate around 1,400 flights daily.

The introduction of air traffic control throughout the world was as a result of the 1922 Paris disaster. On 7th April1922, the pilot for an aircraft dropped below the clouds to be able to look for landmarks, which resulted in a collision in which seven people died. It was therefore decided to introduce radar, radio stations and air traffic control to navigate aircrafts to and from airports. However, these air traffic controllers could only give red or green lights for take – off and acknowledge position reports as sent by radar report. Substantial developments took place as a result of the outbreak of the Second World War, which continued thereafter.

The United Kingdom National Air Traffic Control Services under the then Ministry of Civil Aviation was formed in December 1962 to unify civil aviation and liaise with military aviation. It became a part of the Civil Aviation Authority when it was formed in December 1972. The United Kingdom was divided into two regions, the London Flight International Region covering the whole of the United Kingdom except for Scotland and the Scottish Flight International Region. The London Flight International Region was based in West Drayton (To the west of London a few miles to the north of London Heathrow Airport) until it moved to its present location in Swanwick, Hampshire on 27th January 2002.

In relation to operations at Heathrow, there are two control centres at the air traffic control centre in Swanwick, Hampshire:-
1. 1 The London Area Control Centre which manages air traffic anywhere within the London Flight International Region.
2. The London Terminal Control Centre which handles air traffic to/from London's five airports (i.e. Heathrow, Gatwick, Luton, Stanstead and London City) while below 7,467 metres (24,500 feet). It can be likened to a massive motorway intersection with routes crossing in all directions at multiple levels.

   The United Kingdom follows the International Civil Aviation Organisation System; which classifies airspace in order that pilots anywhere in the world can understand what flight rules apply and the nature of the air traffic control services which are on offer.

3.2 London Heathrow's Air Traffic Controllers

The staff who are based at London Heathrow are part of the staff of the United Kingdom National Air Traffic Control Services.

These controllers have to manage a "fluid jigsaw", orchestrating the landings, take offs and ground movements of aircrafts.

Unlike at the centre in Swanwick where people work purely from radar information, people based at Heathrow rely both on what is on their screens and what they can physically see from their windows.

Staff include a supervisor, a ground movement planner, ground movement controllers (Arriving aircrafts between landing on runway and reaching gate; and departing aircrafts between leaving gate and preparing for take – off), air arrivals controllers (Who ensures the correct minimum space between landing aircrafts and ensures that the runway is available) and air departure controllers (Who ensure the safe take offs of aircrafts).

3.3 Airline Take – offs

Pilots must file a flight plan for each flight containing details including destination, route, timing and height.

Airline departures involve a number of tasks for the pilots:-

1. Upon arrival at an aircraft, the pilots must make various checks to include walking round the outside of the aircraft to ensure that everything is serviceable, checking that all tyres are in good condition, that there are no hydraulic leaks, that all switches and controls are in their correct place, that the computer system is functioning properly, that the air conditioning system is functioning properly and that there are no obstructions..

2. The pilot must be aware of the amount of fuel which will be consumed over the entire flight, taking into consideration, distance to be covered, queuing time for landing at destination, weight of aircraft, wind speed and direction.

3. The pilots then request their slot time with Air Traffic Control (nb Slot times control the numbers of aircrafts in any particular airspace at any one time).

4. Pilots must complete a further check list immediately before take – off to include switching on appropriate lights and warning cabin crew about immediate take off.

5. The pilot needs to know the speed which is required for take – off, taking into consideration the direction and speed of the wind, the size of the aircraft and the weight carried.

6. In anticipation of an abortive take off, the pilots must be aware of the distance within which the aircraft can make an emergency stop taking into consideration the direction and speed of the wind, the size of the aircraft and the weight carried.

7. Once Air Traffic Control give clearance for take – off, ground clearance staff push the aircraft back, after which the aircraft taxis and queues for take – off. Once ground clearance staff push aircrafts back from their stands, aircrafts generally queue and take off on a free flow system (i.e. the air traffic controllers do not release individual flights for take – off once they are at the front of the take – off queue, but send pilots a "pre – note" via a computer system that their flight is pending). This allows the tower controller at the airport to decide the most efficient departure order. The aircraft's standard instrument departure routing does not generally conflict with the sequence of aircrafts approaching the airport or clash with the departures of other aircrafts

8. If a problem arises while on the runway, the pilots must know whether they can abort or they must take off; taking into consideration the speed that the aircraft is moving, the distance to the end of the runway, the direction of the wind and the weight which is being carried. Once take off is completed, the lateral navigation path as programmed into the flight management computer, is followed.

3.4 While in Flight

Aircrafts fly within designated controlled airspace under the supervision of the air traffic controllers, but otherwise pilots take full responsibility for their own safety.

3.5 Landing

Landings have to be undertaken manually and smoothly. A long and continuous descent is always preferable. A crosswind landing is more difficult. The pilots must keep a look out for other aircrafts.

The general procedure for landing:-

1. As soon an aircraft enters the London Flight International Region of the United Kingdom National Air Traffic Control Services, the captain contacts the controllers of this region. This organisation manages the descent to include holding required before it lines up to land.

2. One hour before landing, the pilots request the Automation Terminal Information
Service for relevant information (To include weather conditions, which runways to use, available approaches). One function of this service is to reduce congestion.

3. .Pilots note important factors like the weather, the general terrain, operational constraints, remaining fuel, expected taxi route and designated stand/gate.

4. Pilots also discuss the pre nominated diversion airport with Air Traffic Control in case the aircraft is unable to land at London Heathrow. Enough fuel must be carried for this possibility.

5. .Airlines which are destined for London Heathrow Airport usually enter its airspace through one of four reporting points, known as "stacks" to queue to land:

    5.1 These reporting points are Bovington to the north west over Hertfordshire, Lamboume to the north east over Essex, Biggin Hill to the south east over Bromley and Ockham to the south over Surrey.

    5.2 Each reporting point is defined by a radio navigational beacon.

    5.3 Aircrafts orbit their reporting point or "stack" in an orderly pattern; they enter the "stack" at the top and move down as others leave. Aircrafts are held at between 7,000 and 15,000 feet above ground level at 1,000 feet intervals.

    5.4 When these holds become full, aircrafts are held at more distant points until cleared onward to one of the four main holds.

6 Once the aircraft is at the bottom of the "stack" (Or air traffic is light without any queue for landing) and is able to land, the pilot contacts the air traffic controllers in the airport itself who then take full responsibility for the aircraft. These air traffic controllers manage multiple flights and must ensure safe separation between them.

7 The pilots consider the procedure for a "go around" in the event of a missed approach.

8   The pilot's checklist then includes confirmation of flap settings, speed for landing and how much reverse thrust to use once the aircraft touches down.

9   .It is policy for aircrafts to begin their descents at speeds of200 miles an hour and then descend at a continuous rate and continuous speed to minimise impact on local residents. Aircrafts join their descents at the correct height for the distance involved.

10 The pilots then use stages of "flap" with each stage to change the shape of the wings, to generate more lift and to allow aircrafts to fly at slower speeds as they decelerate to landing speed which is determined by the weight carried (Generally around 172 miles an hour).

11 During taxi, the pilots shut the engines and switch to the auxiliary power unit to provide electricity until the aircraft is stationary with ground power connection. Once the gate is reached, the pilots must confirm that the doors can be opened.

Upon arrival at the gate, the pilots must check for possible hydraulic leaks and oil leaks; over the tyres for possible cuts, wear and tear; and the blades inside the fan engine.

The pilots then complete shutdown and security checklist.

3.5.1 Other Relevant Matters Regarding Operations as Applied to London Heathrow

There are substantial restrictions on flights between 23.00pm and 7.00am.

When the airport is closed overnight, a substantial amount of activity take place throughout the premises. Thorough inspections of the security arrangements have to be made. The safety of all runways has to be inspected and on occasions the surfaces have to be replaced. Deliveries and collections of various forms have to be made almost every night. The cleaning of the premises takes place. Various types of repair have to be made.

Most of the airport's internal roads are initial letter coded, with C in the centre, N in the north, E in the east, S in the south and W in the west.

The Aviation Security Unit of the Metropolitan Police is responsible for policing and security, supported by the army in times of heightened security.

As aircrafts make substantially more noise when taking off then when landing, it is policy to land and take off in a westerly direction (From east to west) to reduce noise levels over London; except when this is not possible because of the speed and/or direction of the wind. In order to be fair to people who live or work beneath the approach, the two runways are used alternately each day for landing and taking off.

To reduce noise when landing and taking off:-
1. After taking off, airlines are required to reach a height of at least 300 metres (1,000 feet) above ground level within 6.5 kilometres (Four miles) from the point they begin moving on the runway. Gaining height as quickly as possible reduces engine power and noise more quickly.
2. Aircrafts make their descents at a continuous rate as opposed flying at a level height and then making a sudden descent, as this reduces the need for engine thrust.

Heathrow Airport is connected to the United Kingdom Oil Pipeline System which pumps aviation fuel from the various refineries around the country to the airport where it is held in large storage tanks located near the cargo terminal on the south side of the airport. From these storage facilities, the fuel is distributed to the various aircraft stands through a series of ring mains via a hydrant pot. The advantages of hydrant fuelling as opposed to by means of a tanker are that fuel can be transferred from the storage tanks to the aircrafts more quickly and the removal of the need to take a large tanker to and from already congested stands. Potentially explosive air and vapour are displaced from an aircraft's fuel tanks via vent points on the aircraft's wings. In addition to providing fuel to the departing airlines, there is also the requirement to fuel the 7,000 on site vehicles for aircraft maintenance, vehicles to tow aircrafts, machinery to load cargo, handle baggage, empty toilets, clear snow, de – ice wings, stock up with catering supplies and buses.

3.6 British Airways
British Airways itself has a scheduled route network covering around 170 different locations in around eighty countries. On average, a British Airways flight departs from an airport somewhere in the world once every ninety seconds, contributing to a total of over 250,000 flights a year carrying over thirty million passengers and 500,000 tonnes of cargo.

Chapter 4
Administration and Control at London Heathrow Airport

The purposes of administration and control at the airport are to minimise the impact of disruptions to daily operations; to notify the control tower of all issues regarding inbound and outbound flights; to co – ordinate emergency responses as required by the police, fire and ambulance services (e.g. Disruptive passenger on a flight, a road traffic accident, or an aircraft in distress); and monitor times taken by passengers passing through security or immigration (nb Arrangements can be made for staff and resources to be re – allocated to reduce passenger waiting time).

Compass Centre is the airport's main head office. It is North West of where the A4 and the Longford Road split. All office administration, management, financial and legal matters are dealt with in this office. It is personnel in I.D. Centre in this office who issue staff passes to both permanent employees and contractors.

Administration includes the runways, the terminals, the fuel depots, the hangars, the fire stations and the control tower.

The Airside Department ensures that airport's infrastructure is in tip top condition from the quality of the runways to keeping bird hazards at bay.

I will now consider the subject of finance. There is the need to consider capital investment, traffic forecasts and revenue. Annual costs in 2014 were £975 million; to include security, maintaining assets, new technology, investment to upgrade airport and ensuring that needs are met. Income in 2012 was £2.3 billion. Aeronautical sources of income include landing charges based on weight and noise (Higher at night), departure fees (Amount depends upon destination) and aircraft parking charges, refuelling and aircraft maintenance. Non aeronautical sources of income include retail shops and services, rentals and advertising.

I will now consider the airport's I.D. Centre which is based in the airport's head office (Compass House). This centre issues over 100,000 passes a year to employees and contractors to allow access to authorised areas unescorted. There is an extensive referencing process and criminal records checks for all Restricted Area Pass applications. Also are temporary passes issued to external suppliers? All I.D. passes are colour coded to determine level of access, which can be anything from all areas to landslide only. There have been 103,000 full J.D. pass holders (i.e. Access to all areas) over the past three years.

I will now consider the airport's stakeholders. Stakeholders include airline companies (Which own and control the airlines, check passengers in, deal with cargo, luggage and passengers), the Civil Aviation Authority (Which controls flight paths and airline routes), the various commercial services (Which provide catering, shops, leisure services and banking), H.M. Revenue and Customs (Which controls import and export of goods), the U.K. Border Agency (i.e. Passport control) and public transport operators (i.e. Rail, tube, bus, coach, taxis, car rental companies, car park operators and hotel shuttle services).

Chapter 5
Airfield Operations at London Heathrow Airport

The range of capability required for airside operations at any airport is determined by its size and volume of traffic. The basic function of these operations is to ensure everything is in "tip top condition" from the quality of the runways to keeping bird hazards at bay. By law an airport must close if no fire cover is available; required to deal with fires both in aircrafts and on the ground.

At London Heathrow Airport, such operations come under the control of the Airside Department based in the airport's head office (Compass house) and the Duty Manager Airside.

The responsibilities of airside operations are:

1. To ensure that runways, taxiways and aprons are fully operational and safe.
2. To monitor airfield lights, signs and markings; to ensure that vehicles move freely and comply with airside driving regulations.
3. To ensure that runways and taxiways are free from debris and bird activity; which could damage the aircraft.
4. To inspect all surfaces.
5. To marshal aircrafts to stands.

All surfaces have to be inspected to include apron area, aircraft stands, airside roads and footpaths; with routine inspections regularly. Detailed inspections must take place every thirty two days and engineering inspections every three months

The safety department, which monitors everything, is located in the middle of the airfield.

There is equipment to ensure proper operations during adverse weather, to include equipment to clear and dispose of snow.

Considerations include fire services, rescue and medical services, faulty aircraft landing and terrorism.

I will now consider aprons and stands. These accommodate aircrafts to load and unload passengers, mail and cargo; to park; to refuel; normal maintenance to be carried out; and to facilitate aircrafts without difficult manoeuvres.

There are 26,000 licensed drivers to deliver baggage, carry out inspections, ferry passengers to/from remote stands operate aircraft pushback tugs, to transport catering supplies, maintenance vehicles and sewerage vehicles

I will now consider the runways:-

1. There are two runways for inbound and outbound flights.
2. They must be of a high quality surface construction to deal with the rigours of a constant stream of large heavy jet aircrafts; which in fact necessitates enough concrete to build a new road between London and Edinburgh.
3. There is the need to watch for debris on the runway, birds are always a hazard and the rubber of landing airlines must be removed.
4. Thirty to forty five minute long runway inspections take place daily before the first aircraft is scheduled to arrive in the morning, to include inspecting all overnight works.
5. Inspections of the runways also take place at least four times a day.
6. Maintenance and resurfacing always takes place at night so as not to interfere with flights.
7. Runways and taxiways need management facilities to ensure that passengers can embark and disembark.
8. The runways at London Heathrow represent some of the most intensively used transport infrastructure in the world; and as such the surface has a finite life expectancy. This means that they have to be completely resurfaced around once every ten to fifteen years; to be carried out with the minimum amount of disruption to airport operations generally. The work on each runway therefore has to be carried out in stages each night over a period of around fourteen weeks. The work has to be scheduled each night to allow sufficient time for the new surface to fully harden.
9. When aircrafts land, their wheels are not spinning and in the time that it takes for the wheels to get up to speed they are dragging on the runways as well as being put under pressure because of the weight of the aircraft. The friction built up causes the rubber to polymerise and then harden on the surface. The rubber therefore has to be removed from the surface.

All birds around the vicinity of the airport are considered to be a threat to aircraft safety because a collision between a bird and an aircraft can have a devastating effect due to the speed of the aircraft:-

1. The Airside Safety Department is responsible for bird control and trains staff to carry out this operation on a twenty four hour a day basis.
2. Grass is kept at a height of 150 to 200 millimetres (Six to eight inches) as this height deters birds:-
   2.1 It limits visibility for birds themselves.
   2.2 It impedes access to the soil and ground surface.
   2.3 Techniques to unnerve birds and make them depart include sounds to unnerve birds, imitating the wing beats of large raptors, people on foot and use of firearms with blanks. Culling is only used as a last resort.

The weather at any one time is a very important matter and the airport must remain in constant contact with the Meteorological Office.

The onset of adverse weather has to be dealt with (e.g. Low visibility, strong winds, heavy rain, frost, ice and snow). The Instrument Landing System is used to control landings during low visibility. There are vehicles and tractors used to clear ice and snow.

Daytime operations are dominated by the continuous flow of arriving and departing aircrafts and the servicing of aircrafts. Overnight operations involve maintenance and repair and necessary changes of infrastructure, to ensure that the airfield is ready at 4.30am for the first flying schedule of the day.

Chapter 6
Airline Operations at London Heathrow Airport

Airline operations at the airport for each flight are under the control of a turnaround manager who is employed by the airline company concerned; who is aware that there is a limited time over which to unload aircraft and prepare aircraft for another departure.

Twenty minutes before scheduled airline arrival, the airline's ground based airline staff under an airline turnaround manager prepare for its arrival; in essence to ready a small army of baggage handlers, refuelers, catering and maintenance staff.

Once the airline lands, the turnaround manager ensures connection of air bridge to cabin door to allow passengers to disembark.

Once the aircraft is stationary and the doors can be opened; baggage and cargo teams empty the aircraft, unload empty catering trolleys, remove all catering waste, collect rubbish and clean and tidy the cabin.

The aircraft is refuelled, engineers perform oil and hydraulic checks and all maintenance takes place. There are pipelines to transport aviation fuel to the airport.

Fresh water supply is provided and lavatories and drainage are dealt with.

In cold weather, aircrafts have to be de iced

A new flight and cabin crew then board; luggage, mail and cargo are loaded. I will now consider the loading of aircrafts:-

General – Blankets, cushions, first aid kits, headphones, newspapers, pillows, seat belt extensions for children, soap, tissues and toilet rolls.

Catering – Crockery, cutlery, drink stirrers, glasses, ice cubes, meal trays, paper cups, soft drinks, teapots, toothpicks and bottles of wine.

Passengers then board the aircraft.

Before departure, it is essential to ensure that loads are evenly balanced and that aircrafts are not over weight

It is essential to determine the balance and weight of an aircraft filled with passengers, baggage, cargo and fuel. It cannot be too heavy to take off and the undercarriage will only support a maximum amount of weight when landing. If the weight is one sided, the aircraft's movements would be limited and the life of the aircraft could well be shortened.

Chapter 7
Baggage

London Heathrow handled around 110 million bags of luggage in 2013, again in 2014, again in 2015, again in 2016 and again in 2017.

The system must manage both peak and off peak periods, to transfer baggage between flights even between different terminals quickly, to keep all items secure and keep track of millions of units of luggage.

I will firstly consider departing passengers:-

1. Passengers check in, the baggage is handed in, details of the flight with a bar code is attached to the baggage by means of a baggage tag and the passenger is given a receipt for each item of baggage handed over.
2. The baggage tag has all of the passenger's flight information by means of the bar code to include destinations and stop overs. The bar code number can track baggage at any time.
3. Baggage passes through a series of automatic bar code scanners, where diverters send bags down routes to end in the relevant airline's baggage make up area. If the bag is amongst the 10% which does not register properly it is transferred to another conveyor to be manually scanned.
4. The baggage is then manually loaded on to loading carts and then transferred to the aircraft for bulk loading.
5. Bags are brought up to the aircraft one by one on a conveyor and then placed in shelves in the cargo hold; or placed in containers on the ground which are then placed into the cargo hold.
6. Bags belonging to transfer passengers are loaded into separate areas in the cargo hold from baggage heading for the baggage claim at the flight destination. A monitor at the sorting station tells handlers which bags are going where.

At the destination; it is easy to keep the bags of transfer and terminating bags separate as bags have already been sorted. Baggage for the destination concerned are removed by airline ground handling staff and then loaded on to carts for transfer to the baggage claim area.

At London Heathrow, transfer passengers frequently transfer terminals. In general passengers disembark faster than their baggage, which means that baggage has to be moved quickly.

Oversize items like bicycles, golf bags and large souvenirs are routed to a separate outsize carousel for both arriving and departing passengers.

There is a baggage tunnel which link terminal five and the central area.

Chapter 8
Cargo Operations (to Include Mail/Post and Live Animals)

Over fifty billion pounds worth of cargo passed through the airport in 2013, again in 2014, again in 2015, again in 2016 and again in 2017; a total of 1,569,000 metric tons in each of these years; to include mail and post. Around 1,500 containers were moved daily in each of these years.

Types of cargo include:-

1. Airmail – Designed to meet the specialised requirements of the world's various postal operators.
2. Constant climate cargo – When a specific temperature is required. There are special refrigerators to keep all such items at their respective temperatures.
3. Constant fresh cargo – Designed to keep perishable goods fresh.
4. Courier – Designed around the quality and speed of deliveries of urgent cargo.
5. Dangerous goods – Transported around the world in the safest possible way under the strictest of regulation.
6. Human remains – A caring and compassionate service ensuring that human remains are treated with utmost dignity and transported with minimum delay. There is a fully operational mortuary.
7. Live animal – The shipment of animals is handled by dedicated staff with experience in this area.
8. Loose items – A general cargo service for a range of cargo requirements.
9. Priority cargo – This freight enjoys priority when speed and reliability are of the essence. There is a special handling centre to deal with such cargo.
10. Secure cargo – Valuable consignments dealt with by relevant staff to meet strict security vetting).

The original cargo building was located along the A4 to the east of the access road to the central area.

In 1958, a new cargo building was opened on the south westerly side of the airport south of the southern runway and the 1947 cargo building was permanently closed.

The airport has twenty two warehouses for cargo, the largest by far of which is the main cargo building.

The main cargo building, which spans the size of six football pitches and has five floors:-

1. Is divided into two distinct areas:-

    1.1 Landside – There are twenty four receiving doors to include two for high security items, eight for intact containers and ten for loose cargo; where importers collect shipments and exporters deliver shipments. Inside the landside area is the consignment store with cages for storage and a sorting area. Freight arrives at the facility either in a state whereby it can be sent on as an intact item, or it may need to be broken down for transportation.

    1.2 Airside – Cargo can be stored in containers – There is an external area for cargo to be moved to and from aircrafts.

2. Once cargo is accepted, it is allocated to one of 8,000 cage storage locations. These I .cages have weight sensors to identify loads which exceed the maximum weight allowed.

3. .Each cage is adjacent to the twenty one kilometre rail track which runs over all five floors linked by two large lift shafts.

4. The weight of freight is balanced around the terminal as a whole.

5. Consignments generally have a storage time of between six and twenty four hours in the terminal.

6. Loads can be worked on until two and a half hours before the scheduled flight departure; but must be transported to the aircraft itself not more than thirty minutes before scheduled departure.

7. Freight is transported between the terminal and aircrafts in Terminal Five along a dedicated access road and between the terminal and aircrafts in terminals in the Central Area terminals through the airport's cargo tunnel.

8. Around 1,500 staff are employed.

9. Cargo is flown to and from over 350 destinations to and from the main cargo building.

There is also a Royal Mail centre next to the cargo building. Outgoing mail is taken to this sorting office from around the country, sorted into different countries and then transferred (By airside tunnel) to the various terminals to be transported to their respective destinations (By British based airlines generally). Incoming mail arrives at the various terminals in different airlines (By airlines controlled by the country of origin generally), is transferred (By airside tunnel) to this sorting office and there sorted into the various locations of the United Kingdom.

Cargo has been transferred between the cargo building and the Central Area by tunnel on the airside since December 1968 (Which in January 1972 became known as the Heathrow Cargo Tunnel). It is not open to the public and is only used by vehicles with security clearance to travel airside. Until December 1968, cargo had to be transported between the cargo building and the Central Area round the perimeter of the airport.

The cargo building is connected to Terminal Five by the Western Tug Road.

The Heathrow Animal Reception Centre is situated near to and works in close conjunction with the cargo buildings:-

1. The centre is effectively the live animal border inspection post at the airport.

2. All animals entering the European Union from outside have to pass through such a post to be inspected and have the necessary veterinary documentation issued.

3. A dedicated team of thirty members of staff operate the centre, which is open twenty four hours of the day 365/6 days of the year.

4. The team received and cared for more them eighty million animals in 2013, again in 2014, again in 2015, again in 2016 and again in 2017; to include in each of these years around forty five million invertebrates, seven million live eggs, twenty eight million fish and 13,000 cats and dogs.

5. It is not uncommon for the centre to play host to tigers, lions, rhinos, kangaroos, fish including sharks, cattle, baby elephants, prized race horses and poisonous snakes.

6. Animals arrive at the centre from all over the world. Animals are reunited with their owners once inspected and having cleared customs.

95% of cargo is transported in the holds of ordinary passenger aircrafts (The preferred option), while 5% has to be transported in separate aircrafts because of the size and weight of the cargo concerned

The most serious challenges to the transporting of cargo are the weather and aircraft delays.

The overall range of cargo is diverse to include lifesaving drugs, fresh fruit, fresh vegetables, fresh flowers, automobile parts, spare aircraft engines, dinosaur fossils, live animals as detailed in the last but two paragraphs and the latest high street fashions.

Chapter 9
Passenger Terminals (Known as Buildings Before April 1974)

The basic purpose of passenger terminals is to enable passengers to transfer between the various forms of outside ground transportation and aircrafts.

It is within terminals that passengers check in, hand their luggage in, pass through security, relax prior to departure, transfer between flights (Whether within the same terminals or between terminals), pass through immigration/customs, collect luggage and use amenities (e.g. Shops and catering establishments). Heathrow spent more than a billion pounds in 2013, again in 2014, again in 2015, again in 2016 and again in 2017 on improvements. Heathrow's terminals can be described as cities in their own rights. They must provide an environment which strikes a balance between the flows of people, providing all necessary information clearly, the needs of airlines, space available to provide amenities and services and security.

The flow of passengers and operations thereon must be managed efficiently. Passengers must be able to pass through ticket checks and screening of possessions rapidly as the time taken does affect reputation; but without compromising the standards of ticket checks or screening of possessions. People pass security screening through more quickly in summer as not wearing large coats; but family groups during the summer holidays can slow matters down.

Terminals need to be safe and secure, to be able to deal with all contingencies and it is essential to ensure that all equipment is operating correctly. Security equipment is serviced, engineering issues are resolved, cleaning takes place, retail outlets are restocked and signage is changed as necessary overnight.

Each of Heathrow's terminals is controlled by a management team, led by an Operations Director and a Terminal Duty Manager. Terminal Five has two Terminal Duty Managers at any one time, due to its size.

These managers have to be able to deal with a large variety of types of emergencies as and when they occur.

One might think that the terminal shuts down overnight, but in fact the period between 23.30pm and 16.30pm is one of the busiest times in the twenty four hour cycle. Security equipment has to be serviced, engineering issues resolved, cleaning takes place, cleaning takes place and when necessary signage is changed. Come 4.30am and everything has to be fully functional for the first passengers of the day.

To ensure the successful construction and opening of a new or re – built terminal:-

1. Consider the need for a new terminal and where it can best be located bearing in mind the natural land terrain, the layout of the remainder of the airport and the nature of the general surrounding areas outside of the airport.
2. Research other terminals, problems which they have experienced and what has been learned.
3. Co – ordination with the remainder of the airport to make disruption elsewhere as limited as possible.
4. Construction to include planning and design of the structures.
5. Once construction completed and the infrastructure is installed, allow a six month period for testing and extensive staff training. There can be as many as 200 trials involving as many as 3,000 people. The baggage system has to be tested at full capacity on numerous occasions to replicate real life operations.

Research has to be constantly undertaken to consider how improvements can be made and problems better solved.

Chapter 9.1
Buildings and Aerodromes Which Have Been Used as If a Part of the Airport but Are No Longer So Used

There are building and terminals which have been used as if a part of the airport but are no longer so used.

The first subject is R.A.F. Northolt. I must first state that this aerodrome has never been a part of Heathrow Airport, at least officially. Between 1919 and 1939, this aerodrome, – together with the aerodrome near Croydon, were the two airports used for public civil aviation. It must be noted that the original aerodrome at Heathrow was constructed during the First World War in 1915 for military purposes, became derelict between 1918 and 1929 and was operational for private aircrafts between 1929 and 1939. As a result of the Second World War, the government expanded Heathrow Airport to its present size in 1944 (So chosen as opposed to other aerodromes because of the nature of the surrounding terrain). After the war, it was determined that Heathrow would be the main passenger airport with R.A.F. Northolt retained for military purposes. However, R.A.F. Northolt continued to be used as an "overspill" for London Heathrow (Generally domestic and short haul international routes) until April 1974.

From 1947, the control tower, passenger building and cargo building were next to each other along the A4 to the east of the present day approach roads to the Central Area. These had been constructed by the Royal Air Force.

I will firstly consider the passenger building:-

1. Facilities were very basic with prefabricated buildings (With the same materials used as for building prefabricated homes) – Passengers, though wealthy, accepted the general facilities though spartan, primitive and basic by to – days standards, as the blitz spirits and attitudes adopted as a result of the Second World War were still prevailing and they regarded flying as a special privilege.

2. Checking in, the departure lounge and area to meet arrivals all in one hall:-

    2.1 The check in counters were on the apron side of the building; the departure gates were on the apron side of the building, passports and boarding tickets checked as passengers exited departure hall for their flights. Times of departure chalked on a giant notice board next to departure gates, staff also called across the hall to call passengers to assemble.

    2.2 As far as arrivals were concerned, all passengers picked their luggage off a trolley on the apron (Next to the building under shelter under cover if rain). Immigration controls for international flights were at the bottoms of the aircraft steps; if wet or very cold inside the aircraft if wet or very cold. Domestic then entered the hall by one of the gates also used for departures, while international passengers used a separate entrance to pass through customs controls.

3. .Passengers walked between the buildings and the aircrafts even if the weather was wet and windy (nb Aircrafts could always be parked on the apron almost next to the doors on the apron side as there were not as many aircrafts).

4. The departure/arrival/meeting hall housed a cafeteria, bar, post office, pillar box and telephone boxes. There were comfortable chairs, small tables and vases of flowers. There was a W.H. Smith and Son.

The air traffic control tower and passenger buildings in what is now known as the Central Area were opened in December 1955. However, this former passenger building was still used for domestic and a few short haul international flights until it was permanently closed in April 1976 following the opening the rebuilt terminal one.

Both Northolt and the pre 1955 northerly terminal handled considerable numbers of movements to include all domestic flights until April 1976.

Chapter 9.2
The Europa and Britannic Buildings (As Known) Between December 1955 and April 1972

The next subject to consider is the Europa and Britannic Buildings (As they were known between December 1955 and 1972). These subsequently became known as Terminals One and Two respectively.

The central area of London Heathrow ort was officially opened by H.M. Queen Elizabeth II for passenger transport on 16t December 1955. The central area was located in the middle of the airport between the parallel runways, with access by means of a tunnel to and from the perimeter road on the northerly side. This 158 acre Central Area housed two passenger buildings known as the Europa Building and the Britannic Building, administrative buildings known as the Queen's Building (Which housed offices), a bus station, car park (Able to accommodate 1,150 cars and twenty coaches) and the 122 foot high air traffic control tower in the centre.

The smaller Europa Building (Terminal One) was located on the north east side and the larger Britannic Building (Terminal Two) on the south east side with the apron was located immediately to the north east, east and north east of these two buildings:-
1. In this way, aircrafts could be parked close to the buildings, so as not to obstruct others arriving or departing.
2. Aircrafts could be parked anywhere on the apron.
3. There was a passenger walkway inside the two passenger buildings immediately next to the apron for passengers to walk to and from the nearest gate to their aircraft; running continuously through both passenger buildings through the Queen's Building; which meant that passengers passing through one building could board and disembark from aircrafts parked at the far end of the other building.
4. As and when aircrafts were not parked next to the buildings, passengers were bussed between the building and their aircrafts.

There were thirty – four gates, each of which were divided in two. Coaches conveyed passengers to and from aircrafts.

For the first time, the arrival and departure areas were on separate levels in each of building; and passengers waited for their departures (In the departure lounges) after passing through passport control. Passengers either walked or were bussed between buildings and aircrafts; depending upon distance between the buildings and the aircraft (There were no walkways or air bridges between airlines and buildings). Departing passengers checked in upon entering the terminal, passed through passport and ticket controls and then waited for their flights in the departure lounge. Immigration (Passport) controls for arriving passengers took place inside the passenger buildings after they had been bussed back from the aircrafts. Luggage for arriving passengers was transported into the terminal building for collection at a point between immigration/passport and customs control. This was the first time on which there was the separation between Land Sides (Checking in, arrivals hall and open to non – travelling passengers) and Air Sides (Only open to travelling passengers whether before or after flights. These new passenger buildings (Unlike the former prefabricated buildings) were modem, spacious and comfortable with smart check in facilities and numerous amenities (i.e. Restaurants, cocktail bars, lounges, hair dressing saloons, post offices, shops and car hire facilities). There were no Victorian frontages to conceal the terminals, offices, control tower and car park; the theme was brick, stone and glass.

There was a public observatory on the roofs of the Queens Building and the two passenger buildings, linked by bridges, access to which was through the Queens Building.

There were no facilities for domestic travel. Domestic passengers either used the 1947/55 terminal or R. A. F. Northolt. The 1947 to 1955 passenger building and R.A.F. Northolt continued to be used as an "overspill" for some short haul international and all domestic flights.

The Oceanic Building (As Terminal Three was then known) facing south west in the Central Area was opened on 13th November 1961 to handle long haul flights. Due to lack of space, British Overseas Airways Corporation and some others remained in the Britannic Building (i.e. Terminals Two) until completion of the north westerly extension at the beginning of 1972.

Due to potential terrorism, all passengers have been searched at security controls since the end of 1971.

Between January 1972 and April 1976, after there was enough accommodation in the Oceanic Building to house all long haul flights, the smaller Europa Building was demolished and re – built. During this time, most short haul international flights used the Britannic Building; while a few short international flights and all domestic flights used the 1947 to 1955 passenger building or R.A.F. Northolt.

Chapter 9.3
Terminal One (Originally Known As the Europa Building)

Terminal One was opened in April 1976. It was located on the north eastern side of the central area on the site of the former Europa building, which had been demolished early in 1972 to make way for this terminal. Excluding piers and air bridges, it was 600 by 275 feet and 45 feet high.

This terminal shared short haul international flights with what had become known as Terminal Two (Formerly the Britannic Building) and was the sole base for all of Heathrow's domestic flights. Upon the opening of this terminal, the post 1947 terminal on the A4 Great Western Road perimeter road was permanently closed and

R.A.F. Northolt was no longer used as an overspill to London Heathrow.

International and domestic flights had separate walkways with aircraft stands, both of which were bi directional.

There is one check in hall for all departure passengers. However, there are separate sets of controls into separate departure lounges for domestic and international passengers respectively.

There are separate baggage collection halls and separate areas of the arrivals hall for international and domestic passengers.

Between April 1976 and April 1986 it was the largest short haul and domestic terminal in Europe.

When Terminal Four opened in April 1986, it was decided that all terminals would be used for both short and long haul international flights, as opposed to having one terminal dedicated to long haul flights.

A further walkway and set of aircraft stands was opened in the international section of the terminal in 1995. As with walkways constructed throughout the world since the 1980s there were separate walkways for arriving and departing passengers.

The terminal covered an area of 74,600 metres between 1995 and 2015.

Following the departure of British Airways from Terminal One in 2008, the terminal was re – designed in order to join the international and domestic departure lounges into one single departure lounge with both security controls available to all passengers using this terminal.

In 2013 there were 13.8 million passengers a year with over 60% domestic or European Union.

Terminal One is at present being demolished and re – built in a design similar to Terminal Five. It closed on 29th June 2015 and is due to re – open in 2020. When the rebuilt terminal re – opens, it will look in many aspects as if Terminals One and Two have amalgamated into a single terminal.

Chapter 9.4
Terminal Two (Originally Known As the Britannic Building)

It was from April1974 that the Britannic Building became known as Terminal Two and only accommodated short haul international flights.

Walkways between the terminal building and aircraft stands and air bridges between gates and aircrafts were built on to Terminal Two between 1974 and 1976.

When Terminal Four opened in April 1986, it was decided that all terminals would be used for both short and long haul international flights, as opposed to having one terminal dedicated to long haul flights.

As Terminal Two had become unserviceable by 2009 and had not been refurbished since it opened in December 1955 (Except to build on bi directional walkways and air bridges between 1974 and 1976), it was decided that this terminal should be demolished (As with the Queens Building) and that a completely new terminal built. When it opened as the Britannic Building in December 1955, it was designed to handle around 1,200,000 people annually; but in its final years of operation it often accommodated around eight million people. Despite the best efforts of maintenance staff and various renovations and upgrades over the years, the building became increasingly decrepit and by 2009 had become unserviceable.

A total of 316,000,000 passed through this terminal between December, 1955 and when it closed in November 2009.

The terminal was designed to accommodate 1 200,000 million passengers a year but numbers of passengers gradually increased subsequent to then and between 2005 and 2008 accommodated some eight million passengers a year.

The terminal was closed on 23rd November 2009 and demolished during the summer of2010.

The building of new terminal involved research, co – operation between all involved, construction, trials and tests prior to opening, baggage system testing and staff training; with airlines moving in over a six month period. Construction of the new terminal building began in November 2010 and it was re – opened on 4th June 2014 at a cost of £2,500,000 – 00. Like Terminal Five, it has a main building but only one satellite building. Its area is 534,470 square feet (49,654 square metres) and there is enough car parking space for 1,340 cars.

The 1955 to 2008 control tower was demolished during the first part of 2013 to make way for new roads to link with the new Terminal Two.

When Terminal One re – opens sometime after 2019, it will look in a number of ways as if Terminals One and Two have amalgamated into a single terminal.

Chapter 9.5
Terminal Three (Originally Known As the Oceanic Building)

Terminal Three (Oceanic Building as known until April 1974) was opened in the Central Area facing south west on 13th November 1961 to handling long haul flights. After Gatwick Airport in 1958 it was the second terminal in the country to use piers and air bridges.

Due to lack of space, British Overseas Airways Corporation and some others remained in the Britannic Building (i.e. Terminals Two) until the opening of the extension in the beginning of 1972.

The extensions to include the increase in the number of piers and air bridges and the new building facing North West to include the new arrivals hall were completed in April 1972. All long haul flights were then transferred to this terminal (As it was to become known from April 1974

The terminal's area is 1,065,220 square feet or 98,952 square metres.

This building had what were then the most up to date facilities. The departure and arrival areas were both at ground level (In separate buildings with internal access between them), unlike the other two buildings where the arrival and departure areas on different levels, with the departure area facing south west and the arrival area facing north west. This was the first passenger building (Other than London Gatwick) I with moving walkways and air bridges between the building and the aircraft. There was a direct indoor link between the check in area in the departure building and the arrival hall.

When Terminal Four opened in April 1986, it was decided that all terminals would be used for both short and long haul international flights, as opposed to having one terminal dedicated to long haul flights.

Terminal Three was refurbished between 2006 and 2007 to include a pedestrianised plaza complete with canopy in front of the building and new levels built above the existing walkways to accommodate arriving passengers (To enable complete segregation between arriving and departing passengers) and the new drop off area outside.

19.4 million Passengers on 104,000 flights passed through this terminal during the course of2015.

It is due to be closed in 2019 for demolishing and re – building, that is after Tenninal One re – opens.

Chapter 9.6
Terminal Four

By the early 1980s annual passenger numbers had increased to thirty million and more terminal space was required. Terminal Four was therefore constructed on the south side of the airport (East of the cargo terminal) and opened on 1st April 1986.

The terminal's area is 1,135390 square feet or 105,481 square metres.

It has direct access to the A30 and Perimeter Road. Like Terminals One and Two, the departure area is on the level above the arrival area. It was the first British terminal with "open plan" waiting areas at the departure gates themselves and to have the walkways for departing and arriving passengers on separate levels. There is a short stay car park next to the terminal.

It was built on the south side of the airport to avoid increasing congestion in the Central Area.

Under original plans, it was to be used for "point to point short haul traffic" due to its distance from the Central Area. It was designed to facilitate the rapid movement of passengers through the building, a requirement for short haul business based flights. Shortly prior to the opening of this terminal, it was decided that all terminals would be used for both short and long haul flights, as opposed to having one terminal dedicated to long haul flights. Whereas arrivals and departures for short haul

flights have been at continuous levels throughout the day, arrivals and departures for long haul flights have been in "peaks and troughs" (i.e. Very quiet at certain times of the day, but many flights to and from different locations around the world arriving and/or departing at virtually the same time of day).

As the terminal was near the cargo building, passengers in transit (When the United Kingdom was neither the point of origin or destination) could be transported by airside buses between the terminal and terminals in the Central Area as required.

Terminal Four was refurbished between June 2008 and 2010. As well as the interior of the terminal, the forecourt was renovated to reduce traffic congestion and improve security.

9.9 million passengers on 62,000 flights passed through this terminal in 2015. Over 73% of flights are to and from non – European Union countries.

Chapter 9.7
Terminal Five

Terminal Five is located on a 260 hectare (640 acre) site at the westerly end of the airport between the western ends of the two runways. There is direct access to/from the perimeter road, the Stanwell Moor Road (Between the A4 near Longford and the A30 near Staines) and the M25.

The terminal itself is the size of Hyde Park, the main building itself is the size of five football fields and it is the largest free standing building in the United Kingdom. The main building 400 metres long, 176 metres high and 40 metres high; and the two satellite buildings 442 metres long, 52 metres wide and 19.5 metres high. It is designed to handle thirty five million passengers a year. The entire area is 300,000 square metres. It is the largest free standing building in the United Kingdom.

The planning process for Terminal Five was very lengthy. Consideration had to be given to the general environment, potential pollution, blight, access to/from the terminal and access between this and the other terminals. The possibility of a fifth terminal emerged in 1982 (Four years before the opening of Terminal Four). Planning studies commenced in February 1988, the proposal for this terminal was formally announced on 15th May 1992 and the formal planning application was submitted on 17th February 1993. The public enquiry began on 16th May 1995 and ended on 17th March 1999 after sitting for 525 days. The government granted planning permission on 20th November 2001.

Construction of the terminal began in September 2002 and it was opened to passengers on 27th March 2008. It was designed by Mr Richard Rogers and cost £4.3 billion to build. The nine tunnels which were required to provide road and rail access and provide drainage, were all completed in January 2005. Putting just the roof of the main building into place took over a year and was completed in December 2005; tall cranes could not be used as these might have obstructed low flying aircrafts; the roof was therefore assembled in segments on the ground and then pumped on small jacks to its position; the roof had to be kept absolutely flat while pumped into its position.

Over fifteen thousand volunteers were recruited for sixty eight trials lasting from September 2007 to March 2008 to test the terminal's readiness prior to its opening.

It became necessary to build a new taller (Eighty seven foot high) air traffic control tower as the existing one did not have "communication" access to this terminal. As the airport had to remain fully open at all times, the tower had to be constructed off the premises and then taken to its location on three trailers and erected its location overnight (The five hours when the airport is closed). It entered service on 21st April 2007.

Two of the most time critical civil engineering sub projects of the terminal's construction were the diversion of the two rivers (i.e. The Duke of Northumberland River and the Longford River) around the western perimeter of the airport and the re – location of the Perry Oaks Sewage Works (On the westerly side of the airport within the perimeter) to Iver South in Buckinghamshire. The diversion of the two rivers involved placing them into two man made channels and the moving and planting of a substantial amount of river wildlife and plants.

As opposed to walkways, this terminal boarding gates on three sides of the main building and two satellite buildings each with boarding gates on all four sides. The second satellite building did not open until 2010 as planning permission was only given in September 2001 and work was delayed as there was then uncertainty as to the effects that the events in New York might have on aviation.

British Airways transferred its entire domestic, most of its international and some of its Gatwick operations to this terminal when it opened as it had sole use.

Glass is used as much as is practically possible:-
1. On the departure level to enable people to view the airport, aircrafts, and countryside in all directions; and the glass roof means natural sunlight in daylight hours.
2. The boarding/disembarking ramps to enable people to see the aircraft they will be or have been travelling on.

International and domestic passengers use the same facilities:-

1. Departing passengers check in/hand over luggage/collect boarding passes without change; pass through security and boarding pass control to enter the departure lounge; there is a single lounge for both international and domestic passengers; and passport control for international passengers travelling abroad is at boarding gates. Passengers who require the satellite terminals will only make their way to the departure gates in the satellite building by means of the shuttle railway once their flights are called.

2. Arrivals – Domestic and international passengers are directed through different routes as soon as they enter the terminal building (nb Staff know whether a flight arriving at a particular gate in a domestic or an international flight) – The route for domestic passengers only involves luggage collection while the route for international passengers also involves passport and customs controls – International and domestic arriving passengers are separated as soon as they enter the terminal building. Those arriving passengers who arrive at the satellite terminals make their way directly to the main terminal via the shuttle railway; where they pass through passport control, collect luggage, pass through customs and leave Terminal.

3. Domestic services use the northerly end of the main building, European services use the remainder of the main building and long haul services use the satellite buildings – The reason is that passengers making shorter journeys generally expect to spend shorter periods of time passing through and waiting in terminals, while passengers on long haul flights generally accept lengthier times passing through and waiting in terminals.

4. The satellite buildings only house departure/arrival gates, all other activities take place in the main building – They are only used by long haul flights and not for short haul or domestic flights.

5. In the main terminal, checking in and security controls take place on the upper/top level. After passing through security control and boarding pass inspection, the departure lounge is on two levels. The lounges for first and business class passengers will be at the southerly end of the higher level. The departure gates (For domestic and European services) are on the lower level. Access to the shuttle railway for the satellite buildings is by means of lifts or escalators from the lower level.

6. In the main building, all Arrival activities will take place on the lower levels (To include collecting luggage; and except for domestic passport and customs).

7. Passengers "In Transit" when both flights use the satellite buildings – Arrive at arrival gates and make way to the main building via the shuttle railway – Make way to the departure lounge where wait until flight is called – Once flight is called, return to the satellite building via the shuttle railway.
8. Direct access between both the Departure and Arrival areas on the Land Side of the main building; and the railway/underground stations, hotels, short stay car parks and shuttle bus services to/from the long stay car parks.
9. The whole complex is fronted on the westerly side by a separate building containing road transport facilities.

The terminal absorbs thirty million passengers a year and has sufficient seating for 9,000 people at any one time.

There are sixty aircraft stands. There are 4,000 car parking spaces.

There are top grade hotels next to this Terminal.

Within the complex are more than one hundred shops and restaurants.

An underground automated rail shuttle is used to transfer passengers between the main building and the two satellite buildings.

The opening of Terminal Five enable the £6.2 billion investment for the remainder of the airport to begin to include the terminal three forecourt, the whole of terminal four and the complete re – building of terminal two.

In 2015 were 26.3 million passengers on a total of 185,000 flights.

Chapter 9.8

Some Features of Passenger Terminals at London Heathrow Airport

I would like to consider three features of the passenger terminals at London Heathrow Airport.

The first matter which I would like to consider is the check in desks:-

1. Terminal One since the completion of its refurbishment in April 1976 until its closure in June 2015 – The check in desks were located in what can best be described "as rows of islands" on the departure level – Problems arose as and when the terminal became busy and lengthy queues formed – It is due to re – open around 2020.

2. Terminal Two – In the building which opened in December 1955, closed in November 2009 and was demolished in 2010; the check in desks were lined against the wall on the ground level; and passengers ascended one level of stairs after checking in before passing through passport/security controls – The new terminal opened in June 2014 with a similar system to Terminal Five (See below).

3. Terminal Three – The check in desks are lined against the wall on the ground level; after checking in passengers ascend one level of stairs before passing through passport/security controls.

4. Terminal Four – The check in desks are lined along a line by the wall on the departure level; either side of passport/security control.

5. Terminal Five – The check in desks are designed in order that passengers walk forwards towards the passport/security control after checking in; as opposed to having to walk round the other queues to the controls (nb The area between the check in desks and passport security controls remains accessible to the non – travelling public).

The second matter which I would like to consider is the walkways and departure gates:-

1. The original walkways and air bridges in Terminal One (Both international and domestic) were installed when it was re – built between 1972 and April 1976, those in
2. Terminal Two were installed between 1976 and 1978 and those in
3. Terminal Three (Installed when as it was built and subsequently extended, completed in 1961 and 1972 respectively); all had/have hi directional walkways and enclosed departure gates (i.e. In enclosed rooms only accessible to passengers for the flight on hand) The second international walkway in Terminal One which was opened in 1995 and the
4. Terminal Four; both have segregated departure and arrival levels and open plan departure gates. The arrival and departure routes amalgamate/separate at the ramp to/from the aircraft. The departure gates are open plan in that there are no walls between these and the departure lounge and departing passengers can in fact occupy seats other than those for one's own flight (Though this is not encouraged). As part of the refurbishment of Terminal Three between 2006 and 2007, a second level of walkways was constructed above the existing level to act as the Arrivals level, thereby completely separating arrivals and departures.
5. Terminal Five which opened in March 2008, the re – built Terminal Two which opened in June 2014 and the re – built Terminal One which is scheduled to open around 2020 do not have walkways. They have a main building and satellite buildings with open plan departure gates round the perimeters.

The third feature is about places of worship. An interdenominational chapel was first proposed in 1965. The St Georges Chapel in an underground vault adjacent to the former control tower in the Central Area was dedicated on 11th October 1968; with Anglican, Catholic, Free Church, Hindi, Jewish, Muslim and Sikh chaplains. Since 2008, there have been prayer and counselling rooms to accommodate all recognised faiths in each terminal, where services have been regularly held at the times appropriate for each faith respectively.

When Terminal One re – opens sometime around 2020, it will look in a number of ways as if the two terminals are a single terminal. Departing passengers still check in within their respective terminals but once on the airside such passengers can move between the two terminals, aircrafts might not necessarily dock in their scheduled terminals and arriving passengers might be routed through either terminal to pass through immigration and for baggage collection. Advantages include:-

1. When overcrowding is one sided between the terminals regarding aircrafts at stands, aircrafts can easily be routed to stands linked to the other terminal.
2. When numbers of arriving passengers are one sided between the terminals, passengers can be directed to the immigration desks and luggage taken to the collection areas in the other terminal.

Chapter 10
Security

The role of security in the future was not realised when the aerodrome was first completed in 1929, security was controlled by the military between 1939 and 1945, security as such was introduced in the last quarter of 1971 because of concerns over terrorism, it was overhauled in September 2001 and it disrupted the 2006 terrorist attempts.

Back in 1950, people were allowed on to the apron tarmac to welcome friends and family on an inbound flight and there was no perimeter fence round the airport. A perimeter fence was initially erected but only to stop people from wandering on to the airport. Nowadays, there is a perimeter fence reinforced to prevent penetration.

Security has been one of the airport's major essential aspects of expenditure, essential to prevent terrorism, protect the safety (Whether passengers, staff, the • airlines, or the buildings).

Security has to be arranged in such a way so as to reduce delay and inconvenience to passengers or operations. It is expensive to the airport as it involves more staff and equipment.

In 2006 it was ruled that no hand luggage was permitted other than essential items like travel documents and medication; but this was subsequently relaxed to

I allow hand luggage and small quantities of liquids.

Security is at present controlled by the Metropolitan Police, the Border Force, airline security and intelligence services, between which co – ordination is essential. There is a Metropolitan Police Operational Command Unit; and an onsite police station with over 400 officers on duty.

The police are armed and have dogs.

Most security is undertaken "in house" with 3,200 employees. I will now consider some of the features of security:-

1. Road layouts are designed to prevent vehicles from building up speed.

2. There is a secure fence round the perimeter which is high, made in ways difficult to scale and which security patrols regularly scan.
3. All conduits, sewers and pipes are secured to prevent penetration
4. There are sixteen official control posts manned twenty four hours a day to provide access to all except passengers.
5. There are over 6,500 security cameras.
6. Car parks are a minimum distances from the terminals.
7. The flow of passengers is designed so as not to create targets.

Security has to deal with airline staff and crew, foreign airlines and foreigners, retail and catering outlet staff, when refurbishment required also contractors and there is a high concentration of people in the terminals.

There is a need to ensure that each employee has access to areas they need but to no more.

Security must not be more intrusive to passengers then necessary and there must be space for passengers to reconcile their belongings afterwards. Passengers have to pass through metal detectors. Carryon items go through an X Ray system; with which there are images on the monitor which allow machine operators to detect items in a luggage bag. Security body scanners reduce the need for metal detectors or full body searches. There are also full body scanners.

There must be clear signage regarding what is allowed both in the hold and as hand luggage.

The screening of hold baggage requires a high commitment of motivated manpower and advanced resources. Enhanced X Ray images analyse the composition and contents of each bag before it is allowed on to an aircraft. Once it is scanned it is held securely until it is safely on board the aircraft. If a passenger does not board the aircraft, the luggage is unloaded.

There are more than 6,500 cameras throughout the airport.

Security personnel require training to deal with all contingencies. They have to be trained in the use of behavioural detection techniques to single out passengers behaving suspiciously, who are subjected to additional security measures or referred to the police or border authorities.

The National Aviation Security Committee, which consists of representatives from the government, the police and the aviation industry as a whole, co – ordinates airport security.

The International Civil Aviation Authority makes recommendations and the European Commission establishes common rules and standards.

Chapter 11
I surface Access

The General Position Between 1918 And 1925

There was no rail access to and from the airport. The underground only went as far as Hounslow West (nb The line to Hounslow West was for all purposes a part of the District Line until 1931 when it became a part of the Piccadilly Line). The nearest main railway line was the line out of London Paddington to Bath, Bristol, Devon, Cornwall, Maidenhead, Reading, Slough and South Wales. The only stations on this line within reasonably close proximity were West Drayton, Hayes and Hartington and Southall, with all local stations only served by the London/Maidenhead stopping service.

There were no motorways, flyovers, road numbering, or road classification throughout the United Kingdom. Roads were either local roads, rural roads, or long distance routes; always known by their names.

Road access requires more consideration:

1. Bath Road between London and Bath ran along the northern borders of the aerodrome – From Knightsbridge, it followed the route of what is now the A315 passing along the southerly side of Hyde Park and Kensington Gardens; then the Royal Albert Hall, then along Kensington High Street, past Holland Park and then Olympia; then through Hammersmith and then along Chiswick High Road – It then went left into what is now Heathfield Road, under the present route of the A4 and then along Wellersley Street and then past the access road to Kew Bridge on the south side (With Kew Bridge station on the north side) – It then continued along what is now the A315 through Brentford and Isleworth to the centre of Hounslow itself – It then followed what is now the A3006 past Hounslow West station to where it joins the present A4 – It then followed the present A4 (nb Near the present access tunnel was the Magpies public house which at one time provided facilities for horse drawn transport and exists to this day). – It then went along what are now unclassified roads through Longford, Poyle and Colnbrook to join the present A4 to the west of Slough for the remainder of its route to Bath.

2. The main road between London and the south west of England left Bath Road in the centre of Hounslow to follow what is now the A315 through Feltham to where it joined the present A30 – It then left the present route of the A30 to pass through Staines and Egham before rejoining again west of Egham.

3. The main road between Kingston upon Thames and Harrow has remained unchanged except between the south east of Hatton and Hayes – It left the present route to the south east of Hatton to continue along Faggs Road to Hatton; then it passed through Hatton; then it ran directly to the present junction between the A4 and A437; then it followed the present A437 through Harlington to Hayes; and then followed what are now unclassified roads to rejoin the present A312 near Hayes. Note – Many of the present routes of the A4, A30, A30, A406 North Circular Road and A205 South Circular Road did exist; but not as through/major routes. However there were no flyovers, there were no bypasses (i.e. Colnbrook, Egham, Hayes, Longford and Staines) and there was no through North or South Circular Road.

The only forms of available public transport were local bus services along Bath Road, the then route between Hounslow and Egham and the then road between Kingston upon Thames and Uxbridge.

Tithe Barn Lane was a small rural lane between Stanwell and Longford around 400 yards to the east of the post 1944 Stanwell Moor Road; and Heath Row Lane was a rural lane between West Bedfont and the Bath Road (Near the Magpies public house which still stands to this day) and Bedfont Road was a local road between Hounslow and Stanwell via West Bedfont.

I will consider road travel to and from the aerodrome prior to 1925:-

1. From Central London, take the Bath Road via Kensington High Street, Hammersmith, Chiswick, Brentford and Hounslow to where it met the present day junction between the A4 and A30. Then take the local road which ran to the south of the aerodrome.

2. From the west, take the Bath Road through Slough and Colnbrook; then the Tithe Bam Lane (A rural lane) to as far as Stanwell, pass through Stanwell and then the local road which ran to the south of the aerodrome

3. From the south west, follow the main road from south west England to London through Egham and Staines, then just before Feltham take the local road which ran to the south of the aerodrome. From Guildford, follow what in 1925 would become the A320 through Woking to Staines, then the same as from south west England.

4. From all other locations, cut across country or outer London to the Bath Road (The London/south west England if from the south west) and follow the routes as detailed.

Developments to Road Infrastructure Into, Out Of. And Around London 1925 To 1930

Roads were numbered and classified throughout the United Kingdom. The present day routes of the A4, A30, A406 North Circular and A205 South Circular were opened as through routes between 1925 and 1930; to include the construction of by – passes round Longford, Poyle, Colnbrook and Egham. There were still no flyovers over this period and no by pass round Staines. It was the local road which passed the aerodrome to the south which over this period was developed as the rerouted A30 main road from London to Staines and the South West of England.

Also developed in similar ways were arterial roads to and from London. Some of the pre 1925 routes retained their former names (e.g. Parts of the pre 1925 route between London and Bath retained the name Bath Road)

The Second World War

The Government expanded the aerodrome for military operations (i.e. For several aircraft's at the same time to land and take off quickly in any direction). It was expanded eastwards, southwards and westwards, basically to what there is at present. It was to be expanded in a south easterly direction almost to Hounslow town centre itself but the war ended in May 1945 before this aspect of the work itself started. It was expanded northwards to as far as the A4 to the south of Harlington.

The A312 was re – routed along its present route between the south of Hatton and Hayes. The stretch between the post 1930 routes of the A30 and A4 had to be closed to make way for the airport expansion, south of the A30 through Hatton became a local road and north of the A4 through Harmondsworth was renumbered as theA437.

Tithe Barn Lane was closed and the village of Perry Oaks through which it passed had to be closed to make way for the airport expansion; and the Stanwell Moor Road was constructed between the A30 at the easterly end of the Staines by pass and Bath Road (Forming a part of the pre 1925 route of the A4) immediately to the west of Longford and to the immediate west of the post 1930 Perry Oaks Sludge Sewerage Disposal Works.

Public Transport Between 1947 And 1955

Between 1947 and 1955, the only available forms of public transport were local bus services along the A4 and taxis – Flying was still very expensive and only available to the "privileged few" who generally either drove their own or hired chauffeurs.

The Central Area When It Opened On 16th December 1955

What has become known as the Central Area of London Heathrow Airport (i.e. Terminals One, Two and the Queens Building) opened on 16th December 1955. It was accessible by a road tunnel from the northerly side of the perimeter road. It housed a local bus station, a coach station, a taxi rank and a car park.

The car park was used for both long and short stay visitors. There were no plans at the time for any other car parking facilities as it was not envisaged that demand for car parking would ever exceed the available parking space.

There were two types of coach services. Coach services between London on the one hand and the west or south west country on the other hand served the airport. There was also a dedicated coach service between the airport and Central London.

New local bus services were introduced which originated from or terminated at the airport (nb Existing bus services were not re – routed).

There were no plans for rail links as it was not envisaged that airport usage would ever justify rail links.

Other Matters In 1955

The Hammersmith Flyover, the Chiswick Flyover and the Staines by pass were opened.

Motorway Access

I will consider motorway access.

The M4 to the north of the airport opened between the Chiswick Flyover and the west of Maidenhead in 1964. The motorway was accessible to the airport by a road link to/from the northerly end of the tunnel which opened in 1965. The extension of this motorway to South Wales was completed in 1971.

The M25 was completed in the 1986. This allowed easier access between the airport and London's other motorways and major routes. Access between the M25 and airport were via the M4 and the link road to/from the tunnel.

The Piccadilly Line Extension

The Piccadilly Line Extension to London Heathrow Airport was opened on 16th December 1977.

The Piccadilly Line was extended from Hounslow West to the Central Area with an intermediate station at Hatton Cross. Construction began early in 1972 and it was opened 16th December 1977. The dedicated coach service to/from Central London was discontinued. The line was hi directional. Non flying passengers with points of origins or destinations to the west or north of the airport could use the Piccadilly Line between Central London and the airport; and then coach services, local bus services, taxis, or other means of travel for the remainder of their journeys.

This subject requires special consideration as the construction of this line to the airport was very much on a piece meal basis.

Long Stay Car Parks Along the Northern Side of the Perimeter Road

As demand for car parking was gradually increasing after 1971, it was decided to construct long stay car parks along the northern side of the perimeter road.

These were completed in the early 1980s after which it was policy only to encourage short stay car parking within the Central Area. Whereas the car park in the Central Area charged by the hour, the long stay car parks along the perimeter charged by the day with the daily price for the long stay price the equivalent of four hours in the short stay car park and discounts in the long stay car park the greater the longer the durations of so parking.

A courtesy bus service which operated frequently was available between the long stay car parks along the northern perimeter and the Central Area.

People using the long stay car parks were allowed to drive along the perimeter between the airport entrance and the car parks (nb Perimeter road closed to the public otherwise)

Terminal Four – Opened 1st April 1986

When terminal Four opened on 1st April 1986:-

1. .The Piccadilly Line was extended also to serve Terminal Four – It remained bidirectional between Hounslow West and Hatton Cross, but then followed a one way clockwise circle serving first Terminal Four and then the Central Area.
2. Local bus services along the A30 also served Terminal Four.
3. The terminal housed its own taxi rank and short stay car park.
4. Courtesy bus services which operated frequently were also available between this terminal on the one hand and the Central Area and the long stay car parks along the airport's northern perimeter on the other hand.
5. Coach passengers still used the coach station in the Central Area and the courtesy bus service between this terminal and the Central Area.
6. Non flying passengers travelling between local areas north and south of the airport; could travel by local bus to/from the Central Area, the courtesy bus service between the Central Area and Terminal Four and local bus to/from Terminal Four.
7. .Road access to/from this Terminal remains via the A30.
8. Upon the opening of this Terminal, the airport's perimeter road was opened to the general public – Before then it was only open to airport staff and otherwise by official invitation.

Rail Link between the Airport and the London Paddington West Country Main Line

The rail link between the main line (Between West Drayton and Hayes and Harlington), the Central Area and Terminal Four opened on 23rd June 1998. This has enabled direct services between the airport and London Paddington to operate. The two services, both of which have operated every fifteen minutes have been the Heathrow Express between London Paddington and Terminal Four only serving the Central Area and Heathrow Connect serving all stations between London Paddington and the Central Area. Travel between the Central Area and Terminal Four is free of charge. People travelling between locations immediately to the north and south of the airport have also been able to use this service between Terminal Four and the Central Area, or this service to/from Central London.

Terminal Five

This terminal, which opened in March 2008, houses a taxi rank, short stay car park, bus station, coach station, underground station and terminus for the Heathrow Express and Heathrow Connect.

There is also a bus terminus and coach stop within this terminal. Bus and coach services either serve this terminal or the Central Area. It is the responsibility of passengers to check which services serve which bus/coach station.

Following the opening of this terminal, there were changes to the rail and underground services:-

1. The Heathrow Express operates once every fifteen minutes daily between London Paddington Terminal Five only serving the Central Area).
2. Heathrow Connect serves all stations between London Paddington and Terminal Four including the Central Area.
3. Underground services serve Terminal Four and Terminal Five on a 50/50 basis. Services for Terminal Five remain bidirectional serving Hatton Cross and the Central Area. Services for Terminal Four continue to use the post 1986 one way system; but wait in Terminal Four as opposed to the Central Area for up to ten minutes as the Central Area can no longer be used as a terminus).

There is direct access between this terminal and the M25 and the Stanwell Moor Road.

A very frequent courtesy bus service operates between this Terminal and the long stay car parks on the northern perimeter.

The Terminal Four loop had to be closed for eighteen months in order to construct the link to Terminal Five from the west of the Central Areas. During this time a courtesy bus service operated between Hatton Cross and Terminal Four. However, as the Heathrow Express/Connect link between the airport and the London Paddington/west country was not completed until the late 1990s when Terminal Five was very much "on the cards", the link to Terminal Five was started which meant that it was not necessary to close any part of the line to construct this link.

Surface Access as in 2018

Having considered the piece meal way in which transport access to and from the airport has developed since there was first an aerodrome on the site, it is a good idea to consider transport access as in 2013.

The first subject to consider is road access:-

1. If one is travelling from Central London, one will want to take the A4 and M4. For the Central Area, one must leave the motorway at the spur road (Junction Four). For Terminal Four, one must leave the motorway at the A312 (Junction three), take the A312 southwards to the A30 and then the A30 westwards to the access road to Terminal Four. For Terminal Five, one must leave the M4 at the M25 (Between Junctions four and five on the M4 and junction fifteen on the M25) and then leave the M25 at the Terminal Five spur road (Between junctions fifteen and fourteen).

2. If of is travelling from the west, one would be on the M4. For the Central Area, one must leave the motorway at the spur road (Junction Four). For Terminal Four, leave the M4 at the M25 (Between Junctions four and five on the M4; Junction fifteen on the M25), leave the M25 at the A30 (Junction thirteen) and take the A30 to the Terminal Four access road. For Terminal Five, one must leave the M4 at the M25 (Between Junctions four and five on the M4 and junction fifteen on the M25) and then leave the M25 at the Terminal Five spur road (Between junctions fifteen and fourteen).

3. If one is travelling from elsewhere, one would travel to and then take the M25:-

    3.1 For the Central Area take the M25 to the M4 (Junction fifteen on the M25) and then the M4 to spur road (Junction four).

3.2 For Terminal Four take the M25 to the A30 (Junction twelve) and then the A30 to the access road for Terminal Four

3.3 For Terminal Five leave the M25 at the Terminal Five spur road (Between Junctions fourteen and fifteen).

4. For road access between the Central Area, Terminal Four and Terminal Five on the Land Side, use the perimeter road between Terminal Four, Terminal Five and the access tunnel to/from the Central Area.

There is a rail link between London Paddington and the airport. It leaves the main London/Bristol/South Wales line at a point between Hayes and Harlington and West Drayton. From London after passing through the Central Area, the line splits into two, one for Terminal Four and the other for Terminal Five. These services are free of charge for travel between the Central Area, Terminals Four and Five

1. Heathrow Express – Once every fifteen minutes express between London Paddington and Terminal Five only serving the Central Area. Services to/from London Paddington take fifteen minutes to/from the Central Area and twenty one minutes to/from Terminal Five.

2. Heathrow Connect – This service operates once every fifteen minutes, serving all stations between London Paddington and Terminal Four. The service takes twenty seven minutes between London Paddington and the Central Area (Thirty three minutes for Terminal Four). This service was absorbed into Transport for London on 20th May 2018 ahead of it becoming a part of Crossrail in December 2018. (nb Passengers from London Paddington to Terminal Four take the Heathrow Express to the Central Area and change. Passengers from intermediate stations to Terminal Five take the Heathrow Connect to the Central Area and change).

London Underground Access is provided by the Piccadilly Line which runs between Cockfosters, Central London and then either the airport or Rayners Lane/Uxbridge – The Rayners Lane/Uxbridge services use a separate route west of Acton Town – All airport operate bidirectional between Cockfosters and Hatton Cross and alternate between Terminals Four and Five:- The service takes between forty and seventy minutes between Central London and the Central Area:-

1. Terminal Five services – Operate bidirectional between Hatton Cross, the Central Area and Terminal Five.

2. Terminal Four services – Follow a clockwise one way route Hatton Cross, Terminal Four, the Central Area and Hatton Cross – Services wait in Terminal Four for a maximum of ten minutes as they have to use this station as if the terminus (nb Passengers travelling to the Central Area are advised to use Terminal Five services as these run directly, while Terminal Four services follow the indirect route via Terminal Four where they wait in for up to ten minutes. Passengers travelling from the Central Area use either service as they both use the same direct route to Hatton Cross eastwards.)

The next option to consider is access to coach services. There are coach stations in the Central Area and in Terminal Five, but not Terminal Four. It must be noted that coach services only serve one of the coach stations and that passengers are personally responsible for checking which coach station to use. Many coach services to/from the south, south west, west, north west and north of London detour to serve one of the airport's coach stations. Passengers use rail or bus services (See previous two paragraphs and the next paragraph) to travel between Terminals Four, Five and the Central Area as necessary. This includes non – flying passengers local to Terminal Four or for whom the airport coach stations are the most convenient ones for them.

I will now consider access to bus services. There are bus stations in the Central Area and for Terminal Five but for Terminal Four. It must be noted that most bus services only serve one terminal and it is the responsibility of passengers to check which bus station to use. Numerous bus services operate along the A4 past the entrance of the Central Area (nb One changes to a different bus to access the Central Area). All bus services which operate along the A30 to the south of the airport also serve Terminal Four. All bus services are free of charge along the stretch of the perimeter road between Hatton Cross, Terminal Four and Terminal Five and between the Central area and the A4. (nb Bus services serving one of the bus stations are listed at the end of this chapter)

The next subject to consider is travelling by Car and Car Parking:

1. One can only stop a car directly outside of a terminal or in terminal forecourts to set down passengers and their luggage but one is not allowed to wait. Only Licensed
   London taxis and service vehicles (To include the police, customs, emigration and the airport authorities themselves) can be parked unattended directly outside of the terminals. Those meeting arriving passengers must park their cars in the short stay car park and meet their passengers in the arrivals hall.

2. Car Parking:-
   2.1 Since 1980, it has been policy to reserve car parks inside the Central Area and near Terminals Four and Five for "short stay parking" (i.e. To take people to and collect people from the airport and to make short visits) People will be allowed sufficient time to be able to arrive at the terminals in good time and also accommodate airline delays when collecting passengers).

   2.2 .Long stay parking has been located near the perimeter road on the northerly side with regular shuttle bus services between these car parks and the terminals.

   2.3 There are over 22,900 car parking spaces; both long and short term.

3. Car Hire – Foreigners visiting the United Kingdom (And people from elsewhere in the United Kingdom visiting London) might want to rent a car – Car hire operators are located near the perimeter road on the northerly side of the airport – Customers use the shuttle bus services between the car hire firms on the one hand; and the Central Area, Terminals Four or Five on the other hand.

4. If there are several people using a car (i.e. Car rental or parking car in long stay car park), it is acceptable for one person to collect or return/park the car and drive via the terminal to drop off/collect everyone else.

Many people use chauffeur driven cars or taxis

1. Chauffeur driven cars – Passengers are dropped of directly outside of the departure levels of terminals. When chauffeurs meet arriving passengers, they park their cars in short stay car park, meet passengers on the Land Side of the terminals; and passengers either accompany their drivers to the short stay car park or wait outside the terminal for the chauffeur to collect their cars.

2. Licensed London Taxis – Licensed London taxis drop departing passengers directly outside of the departure levels of the respective five terminals; and then move to in taxi ranks directly outside of arrival levels of one of the five terminals to wait for other arriving passengers

There is a free of charge airport controlled shuttle service for passengers taking cars to and collecting car from the long stay car parks and car rental firms:-

1. Buses drop off at and collect passengers directly from outside of terminal buildings.

2. There are numerous bus stops throughout the long stay car parks and within close proximity of all car rental firms in order that passengers do not have to walk far to/from bus stops.

3.There are two services, one for the Central Areas and one for Terminals Four and Five. The buses will call at all of numerous the bus stops in the long stay car parks and near the car rental firms to collect passengers. The bus circuit is that:-

3.1. The Central Areas – The buses drop passengers off outside of the departure levels of each of the three terminals; then drive round the terminals again to collect passengers from the arrival levels of each of the three terminals.

3.2. Terminals Four and Five – The buses first drop passengers off at the departure level of Terminal Five and then on to the departure level of Terminal Four; then drive down to the arrival level of Terminal Four to collect passengers; and finally continue to the arrival level of Terminal Five to collect passengers.

Then drop off passengers as requested at the numerous bus stops in the long stay car parks and near the car rental firms (nb Will not collect passengers at this stage).

The Personal Rapid Transport System, which opened in April 2011, links Terminal Five to the business car park and is used by eight million people a year (7,570,000 long stay and 430,000 short stay). The car parking is within the airport boundary and is both secured and monitored. There are twenty one transport pods, each capable of accommodating four adults – together with two children and luggage. A similar system to link the Central Area was proposed in 2014, but has been deferred due to practicalities and other priorities.

As in 2016:-
1. 30% of all airline passengers use private car; of which total 74% are dropped off at the forecourt or met upon arriving; 19% use the long stay car parks and 7% park away from the airport.
2. 2.12% use scheduled bus and coach services
3. 3.25% use taxi services.
4. 4.27% use rail and tube services
5. 5.6% use hotel shuttle, hire car, or charter bus.

The traffic desk, which is based in the airport's headquarters:-
1. 1 Must remain aware of the road network and the current position therein regarding the road network both inside and outside of the airport perimeter, in particular the road tunnels and vehicle breakdowns cause queues.
2. Must remain aware of road traffic accidents, road closures, diversions.
3. Monitor all car parks, the de – icing of roads and overweight vehicles.
4. Must deal with all issues quickly as could impact on supplies, passengers and staff.

Bus Services as in 2017

Central Area (*Not Controlled By London Transport)

75*	Heathrow, Langley, Slough and Maidenhead
76*	Heathrow, Langley, Slough and Chippenham
105	Heathrow, Harlingham Comer, Southall and Greenford Station
111	Heathrow, Harlingham Comer, Hounslow East, Hounslow, Hanworth Hampton, Hampton Court Palace and Kingston upon Thames
140	Heathrow, Harlington Comer, Hayes and Hartington Station, Northolt Station, Harrow and Harrow Weald
285	Heathrow, Hatton Cross, Feltham, Teddington and Kingston
441*	Heathrow Central, Heathrow Terminal Five, Ashford, Staines and Engleford Green
555*	Heathrow, Hatton Cross, Ashford, Sunbury Village, Shepperton and Walton on Thames
724*	Heathrow, Uxbridge, Watford, Hatfield, Welwyn Garden City, Hertford and Harlow
A10	Heathrow, Stockley Park and Uxbridge
A40*	Heathrow, Uxbridge, Beaconsfield and Hugh Wycombe
U3	Heathrow, West Drayton, Brunei University and Uxbridge
X26	Heathrow, Hatton Cross, Kingston, Sutton and Croydon
N9	Heathrow, Hounslow, Chiswick, Hammersmith, Kensington, Trafalgar Square and Aldwych

Terminal Four (*Not Controlled by London Transport)

Terminal Four is served by a number of local bus services operating between locations south east, south west and south west of the airport.

Bus services 482 and 490 begin from or continue to Terminal Five Otherwise one makes oneself to or from the Central Area or Terminal Five.

Terminal Five

60*	Heathrow, Wraysbury, Datchet, Slough, Eton and Eton Wick
71*	Heathrow, Staines, Egham, Windsor and Slough
77*	Heathrow, Langley, Slough, Windsor and Dedworth
78*	Heathrow, Langley, Slough and Britwell
350	Heathrow, West Drayton, Stockley Park, Hayes and Hartington Station
423	Heathrow, Longford, A4 Bath Road, Hatton Road, the Northern Perimeter Road, Eastchurch Road, Hatton Cross and Hounslow
441*	Heathrow, Stanwell, Staines, Egham and Englefield Green
482	Heathrow Terminal Five, Heathrow Terminal Four, Hatton Cross, Hounslow West, Heston and Southall
490	Heathrow Terminal Five, Heathrow Terminal Four, Feltham, Twickenham, Richmond and North Sheen
N9	Heathrow, Hounslow, Chiswick, Hammersmith, Kensington, Trafalgar Square and Aldwych

Chapter 12
Miscellaneous Matters Relating to the Airport

Ancillary Development
1. The A4 Great West Road with dual carriageway and the Great South West Road (A30) were completed in 1930. These roads enabled fruit and vegetables to be transported speedily to Covent Garden.
2. The Hammersmith and Chiswick flyovers were completed in 1955.
3. There have been hotels on the northern perimeter since 1959.
4. The M4 spur road opened on 23rd March 1965
5. Little was done to improve the roads between March 1965 and October 1986.
6. The M25 was opened on 29th October 1986 (nb The M25 spur road to/from the airport opened in August 1982).
7. There are also hotels also next to Terminal Four and Terminal Five.

Animal Reception Centre
1. The animal reception centre, which is on the south side of the airport, employs thirty staff.
2. Each year there are 80 million animals (To include some 13,000 cats and dogs, 7 million live eggs and 28 million fish.
3. It is the animal border control – If animals come from outside of the European Union, veterinary documents are required and the animals are inspected – If these are not satisfactory, the animals concerned must be quarantined.

Engineering

Many duties and skills required are unique to London Heathrow as:-

1. There are diverse equipment systems and technology to include lifts, escalators, manholes, water mains, aviation fuel pipelines, water transport systems, electricity cables, lighting, ventilation, fire pump stations and sewerage plants.
2. Reliable and accurate data on infrastructure are required at all times.
3. Relevant information must be provided to contractors.
4. All emergencies must be responded to.
5. A pollution control system must be maintained.
6. It is essential to ensure that there is sufficient power across the airport.

Maintenance

Maintenance must always be undertaken at night; which involves repairs and upgrading of infrastructure and facilities; whether runways, stands, or taxiways.

Retail and Catering Outlets

A total of 52,000 square metres is devoted to the 340 retail and catering outlets. A total of 26,000 cups of tea and 35,000 cups of coffee are supplied a day, 700 muffins and 1,800 sandwiches a week and 990,000 kilograms of chips a year. Breakfast is the most popular meal with five million eggs, 6.4 million croissants and 4.5 million rashes of bacon a year.

Signage

Clear and accurate signage is essential to lead passengers through terminals, particularly those who do not travel regularly and foreigners from abroad visiting the United Kingdom for the first time – Different terminals have different layouts; whether with walkways and air bridges; or like Terminal Two since June 2014 and Terminal Five with gates round the main building and two satellite buildings linked by a train – Passengers need to learn how long checking in and passing through security take and how long it takes to walk from the lounge to the departure gate.

VIP Suites

1. The Royal Suite on the southerly side with its own stand was opened in 1991.
2. The V.I.P. suites adjoining the respective terminals are the Hillingdon Suite for the Central Area, the Spelt home Suite for Terminal Four and the Windsor Suite for Terminal Five.

Ground Transport

In 2017, 12% of passengers were taken by car to the airport and dropped off or collected at terminal forecourts or the short stay car parks, 13% of passengers used their own cars and used the long stay car parks, 5% of passengers used their own cars and parked off site, 16% travelled by taxi, 27% used rail services, 12% used bus or coach services, 5% used hotel shuttle, 3% by charter bus and 7% by hire car.

Car Parking

Around eight million people used the airport's car parking facilities in each year between 2009 and 2017; all facilities which are secure or monitored. The short stay car parks attached to the terminals charge by the hour and the long stay car parks on the north side of the airport charge by the day. The rate for parking in the short stay car park for four hours is almost the same as one day in the long stay car park; and discounts are offered to people who use the long stay car park for longer than three days, the longer period of the parking the greater the discount.

Chapter 13
The Piccadilly Line to and from London Heathrow Airport

The Piccadilly Line to and from London Heathrow Airport requires special consideration as its construction has been very much on a piece meal basis.

As I am interested in transport systems as a whole generally and therefore also interested in trains and railways, I will within this chapter appear to be "going off at a tangent" as it might look as if I am writing more about trains and railways.

When railways were first constructed during the first half of the nineteenth century, they were constructed to and from but nothing round or across London, I mean what was then regarded as London. At that time, what was regarded as London was a circle bordered by the River Thames between Tower Bridge and Battersea Bridge, an imaginary line between Battersea Bridge and Victoria, the northerly half of what would in time become the circle line between Victoria and Aldgate and an imaginary line between Aldgate and Tower Bridge. Railways were not built within this circle as the area was almost wholly built up, land was expensive and tunnelling not an option as there was no way to move trains other than by steam engines. Charing Cross, Blackfriars and Canon Street stations were only just inside what was then regarded as London, in order to provide stations on the London side of the river.

Two railway companies, which were completely independent of each other, were formed which decided to build railways either side of what was then regarded as London and continue to/from locations within the London conurbation. Both railways were built north of the River Thames. Around the central areas much of the railways were in tunnel as the buildings above were already in place, but with regular breaks in the tunnels, as all trains were steam hauled.

1. 1The London Metropolitan Railway Company built railways between Aldgate and Whitechapel in the east; and Amersham, Hammersmith, Watford and Uxbridge in the west; basically the routes of what have since become known as the Hammersmith and City and the Metropolitan Lines. These lines were below ground mainly in tunnel between Aldgate and Whitechapel in the east and Finchley Road and Paddington in the west and north west.

2. The Metropolitan and District Railway Company constructed its railway in a number of stages. The stretch between Whitechapel and Earls Court was completed in 1868, the extensions between Baling Broadway and Richmond between 1869 and 1879; the extensions between Edgware Road and Wimbledon between 1880 and 1889; the extensions from Acton Town to Hounslow Barracks (As Hounslow West was then known) and Rayners Lane between 1883 and 1884; and the extension to Barking and Upminster between 1884 and 1902.

This was at a time that there were no technologies to move a train any way other than with a steam operated locomotive. Electrification, multiple units and deep level tunnelling were "well over the horizon; and any form of human travel by aviation (Other than by means of a balloon) were "all well over the horizon".

What would become the Circle Line in 1933 was a joint venture between both companies completed in 1884. It involved constructing lines between High Street Kensington and Gloucester Road and between Tower Hill and Aldgate. Both companies provided trains, fares were retained by the owner of the station where paid.

Electrification of the entireties of both railway networks took place between 1903 and 1905.

The Great Northern, Piccadilly and Brompton Railway Company constructed its deep level railway between Northfields and Finsbury Park between 1906 and 1912; and the extension to Cockfosters was completed in 1933. The line was above ground between Barons Court and Northfields; which meant that there were four tracks along this stretch, two for this company and two for the Metropolitan and District Railway Company.

The whole of what subsequently became known as the London Underground, together with London's bus network were all nationalised under the newly formed London Passenger Transport Board on 1st July 1933:-

1. The lines previously owned by the Metropolitan and District Railway Company became known as the District Line, the lines owned by the Metropolitan and District Railway Company became known as the Metropolitan Line with the route between Whitechapel and Hammersmith subsequently known as the Hammersmith and City Line, the Circle Line became known as such and the lines owned by the Great Northern, Piccadilly and Brompton Company as the Piccadilly Line.
2. This Board then determined that the Hounslow West (As it had since become known) and Rayners Lane extensions would form a part of the Piccadilly as opposed to the District Line.
3. However, District Line trains continued to serve Hounslow West and Rayners Lane during commuter periods only until 9th October 1964 (i.e. Mondays to Fridays either scheduled to arrive in the centre of London between 8.00am 9.45am, or to depart from the centre of London between 17.00pm and 18.45pm.

The aerodrome, which in the course of time became London Heathrow Airport, was constructed solely for military purposes in 1915, closed in November 1918, was re – opened for private aircrafts in 1929, was extended to its current size between 1944 and 1945 and became London's main passenger airport in 1946. There were no plans for it to become London's main passenger airport until the end of the Second World War in 1945. It was not until1968 that extending the Piccadilly Line into the airport was considered, as it was only then that it was thought that usage of the airport would increase to an extent which would justify such an extension.

Construction of the Heathrow extension to the Central Area with an intermediate station at Hatton Cross started in January 1972. The extension was opened as far as Hatton Cross on 19th July 1975 and to the Central Area, on 16th December 1977. (nb Terminal Four did not open until the mid – 1980s). The central area station was then known as Heathrow Central Station.

The Terminal Four loop was completed at the same time as the terminal itself on 1st April 1986 – Trains from Central London remained bi directional between Cockfosters, Central London and Hatton Cross, but went in a one way clockwise loop Hatton Cross, Terminal Four, the

Central Area and back to Hatton Cross. The station in the central area was re – named "Heathrow Terminals 1, 2, 3" and the terminal four station as "London Heathrow Terminal 4". "London Heathrow Terminals 1, 2, 3" continued to be regarded as the terminus in that tube crews changed and tubes were held there for up to ten minutes.

A spur line to Terminal Five had to be constructed in time for its opening in March, 2008. The railway loop via Terminal Four had to close between 7 January 2005 and 17th September 2006 to construct this spur line, during which time trains ran bi directional between Hatton Cross and the Central Area and shuttle buses served Terminal Four from Hatton Cross bus station. Briefly in September 2006, the line terminated at Hatton Cross with shuttle buses to and from the central area while the track configuration and tunnels were altered (nb The Heathrow Express did not close as Terminal Five was "on the cards" when it was opened and the junction and beginning of the spur line to that terminal had therefore been started).

Since the opening of Terminal Five in March 2008 tubes have either been bi directional serving Hatton Cross and the Central Area, with London Heathrow Terminal Five as the terminus; or followed the Terminal Four route serving Hatton Cross, London Heathrow Terminal Four, the Central Area and back to Hatton Cross. Trains serving Terminal Four treat that terminal as the terminus in that crews change and trains might wait in the station for up to ten minutes. The Central Area station could no longer be used as a terminus due to the bi directional line to and from Terminal Five.

Hounslow West Station

Hounslow West Station should also be given some consideration. It is located in the London Borough of Hounslow. When it was opened on 21st July 1884 as one of the terminuses to the Metropolitan and District Railway Company, it was known as Hounslow Barracks in reference to the army barracks on Beavers Lane to the south of the main Bath Road. The main station was Hounslow Town (As it was then known) with the line extended to take account of the army barracks. As Hounslow East Station had not been built, there was no station between Hounslow Town and Osterley. All trains were steam hauled which meant that Heathrow Barracks (As it was then known) required all of the facilities for a terminus served by steam trains. As the station was a terminus, the line changed from a westerly to a southerly direction just before the station in order to be at right angles to the main road outside, as with all other railway terminuses. Also as it was a railway terminus, there were substantial railway sidings. The main road outside was and has since then remained known as "Bath Road" as it was then the main London/Reading/Bath/Bristol road until 1925.

As mentioned all sub surface lines were electrified between 1903 and 1905 and Hounslow West station has been a part of the Piccadilly Line since the whole of the underground network was nationalised on 1st July 1933. Hounslow Central and Hounslow West were re – named as such on 1st December 1925. Hounslow East Station was opened in May 1909. The station building was knocked down and re – built in a design reminiscent of the design then used for other above ground stations in 1931.

Work began on the extension of the Piccadilly Line to London Heathrow in 1972.

As continuing the railway directly beyond the existing platforms would have involved substantial residential demolition, would have routed the railway away from the airport initially and would have involved re – laying the track and platforms at a lower level to go under the main road with the main road still operational; the line was re – routed with new below ground platforms to reduce the demolition substantially and point the railway in the direction of the airport. New below ground platforms had to be built as the line was re – aligned in a westerly direction from outside of the station. The new platforms were adjacent and to the north of the fonner three platforms and access from the existing station building was by means of an extension (nb Extension built in a way in keeping with the immediate locality) The new platforms were brought into use on 14th July 1975, five days before the line was opened as far as Hatton Cross.

The station building had a preservation order which meant that the building could not be altered or re – located and its character could be interfered with. The station entrance, ticket office and barriers therefore remained unchanged; there was an above ground but covered over walkway between this building and the new station in keeping with the locality; and passengers descended down to and ascended from the platforms via a staircase which was immediately above the platforms.

Almost all of the former railway sidings were converted into a car park in 1975; with a half of the area given over to a car boot sale on Saturdays and Sundays between 7.00am and 15.00pm.

DIAGRAM VI – HOUNSLOW WEST STATION
Hounslow Barracks(West) Station Pre 1903

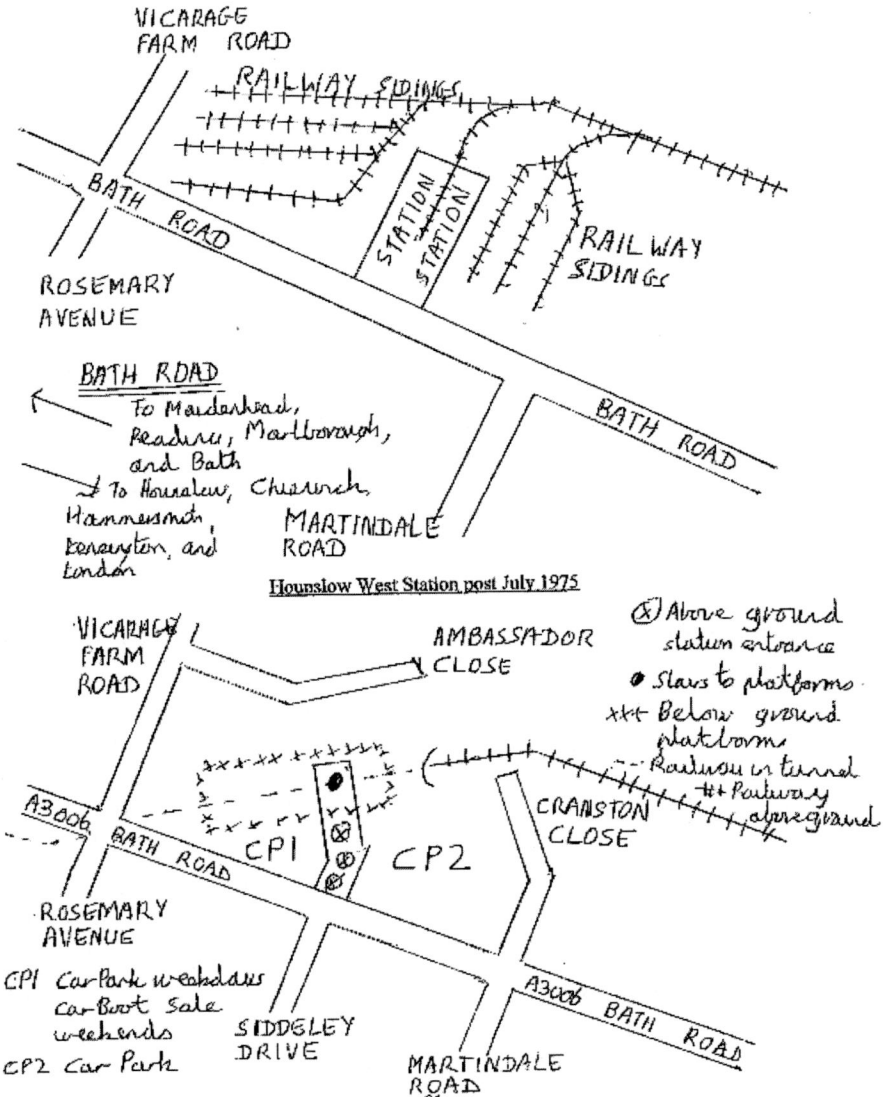

VICARAGE FARM ROAD

RAILWAY SIDINGS

BATH ROAD

STATION STATION

RAILWAY SIDINGS

ROSEMARY AVENUE

BATH ROAD
To Maidenhead, Reading, Marlborough, and Bath
To Hounslow, Chiswick, Hammersmith, Kensington, and London

MARTINDALE ROAD

BATH ROAD

Hounslow West Station post July 1975

VICARAGE FARM ROAD

AMBASSADOR CLOSE

A3006 BATH ROAD

CP1   CP2

CRANSTON CLOSE

ROSEMARY AVENUE

CP1 Car Park weekdays Car Boot sale weekends
CP2 Car Park

SIDDELEY DRIVE

A3006 BATH ROAD

MARTINDALE ROAD

X) Above ground station entrance
• Stairs to platforms
xxx Below ground platform
-- Railway in tunnel
#+ Railway aboveground

127

Chapter 14
Passengers Passing Through London Heathrow Airport

Departures

1. One must know from which terminal one will be departing.
2. Making ones way to the departure area of the terminal:

   2.1 Passengers who are taking their own cars to the long stay car park, or are returning rental cars to their respective rental companies – Take car to long stay car park or car rental company, all of which are located around the northern perimeter of the airport – Then take shuttle bus (Free of charge) from the nearest shuttle bus stop to be dropped off directly outside of the departure area of the terminal from which one will be travelling.

   2.2 Passengers travelling by coach – Will be dropped off in the Central Area (Near Terminals One, Two and Three) or Terminal Five – When travelling to/from a terminal not served by ones coach service, take Heathrow Express or Heathrow Connect (Both free of charge for travel between terminals) to one's terminal (Local bus also free of charge if travelling from Terminal Five to Terminal Four).

   2.3 Passengers travelling by bus – Either:-

      2.3.1   As for "2.2." (i.e. Coach).

      2.3.2   Local bus services passing along the A30 (In both directions) south of the airport also serve Terminal Four (First to drop off passengers outside of the Departure Level and then to the Arrival Level to collect passengers) – If using any other terminal, take the Heathrow Express/Connect to the Central Area or another local buto Terminal Five (Both of which are free of charge).

   2.4 All other passengers make their way directly to departure areas of their terminals.

3. Check in, hand luggage in, collect boarding pass – Passengers travelling business or first class have separate virtually queue free check in counters.
4. Make way through ticket, security and passport (International only) controls to departure lounge – Security involves the use of a full body scanner; passengers who object can have a manual search in a private room – Passengers travelling business or first class have separate "fast track" route.
5. Wait in departure lounge – Shops, catering and seating areas – Also lounges for passengers travelling first or business class.
6. Make way to departure gate once flight is called – Passengers travelling first class allowed to board last, but are given boarding priority when they arrive at the gate before others have boarded.

Arrivals

1. Passengers disembark from aircraft – Passengers who have travelled first class are allowed to disembark first, followed by passengers travelling business class.
2. International (Not Domestic) passengers pass through passport control – Passengers who have travelled first class have a separate "fast track" route.
3. Collect luggage from the Luggage Reclaim Area – The luggage of passengers who have travelled first class will have been unloaded first, followed by business class.
4. International (Not Domestic) passengers pass through customs.
5. One then leaves the terminal:-
   5.1 Passengers collecting their own cars or renting cars from one of the car rental companies – Take shuttle bus (Free of charge) from directly outside of the arrival area of the terminal to the shuttle bus stop nearest to their car in the long stay car park or to the company from which one will be renting (All located around the northern perimeter of the airport –) – Collect car.
   5.2 Travelling by coach – All coaches depart from the Central Area or Terminal Five. When travelling from a terminal if not served by ones coach service, take Heathrow Express or Heathrow Connect (Both free of charge for travel between terminals) to one's coach station (Local bus also free of charge if travelling from Terminal Four to Terminal Five).
   5.3 Travelling by bus – Either:-
      5.3.1   As for "5.2." (Coach)

5.3.2 Local bus services passing along the A30 (In both directions) south of the airport also serve Terminal Four (First to drop off passengers outside of the Departure Level and then to the Arrival Level to collect passengers) – If using any other terminal, take the Heathrow Express/Connect from the Central Area or local bus from Terminal Five (Both free of charge).

5.3.3 All other passengers make their way directly from the terminal.

Non Flying Passengers Using the Airport as an Interchange

Point of origin or destination may be within close proximity of the airport; a convenient location to collect/drop off people using public transport (Heathrow Express, Heathrow Connect, Piccadilly Line, local bus, or national coach service; or change mode of public transport (i.e. Between rail, underground, coach or local bus).

1. If point of origin or destination within close proximity of the airport, travel to/from Central Area, Terminal Four or Five, whichever is the nearest.

2. If collecting/dropping off people changing to or from public transport – Rail and underground serve all terminals – Coaches either serve the Central Areas or Terminal Five; while different bus routes serve the Central Area, Terminal Four, or Terminal Five (nb One can use the Heathrow Express/Connect between the Central Area and Terminals Four or Five; or local bus between Terminals Four and Five; both of which are free of charge).

3. If changing mode of public transport – Underground and rail serve all terminals, coaches either serve the Central Area or Terminal Five, while many bus services serve the Central Area, Tenninal Four, or Terminal Five – Heathrow Express/Connect between the Central Area and Terminals Four or Five and local bus between Terminals Four and Five; all free of charge.

Chapter 15
The Naming of the Airport

The aerodrome's name has changed on several occasions since its initial construction back in 1915.

At different times between 1929 and 1945, the aerodrome has been known as the Great Western Aerodrome or the Harmondsworth Aerodrome.

The aerodrome was first referred to by the name of Heathrow as a hamlet (An isolated row of cottages) on Hounslow Heath located near where Terminal Three is now sited had to be demolished when it was expanded between 1940 and 1945.

The airport was known simply as London Airport between 1946 and January 1972 with the central area known as London Airport Central and the original 1947 terminal known as London Airport North from 1955. Basically it was the only airport in the London conurbation (Within the County of Middlesex until April 1965 since when been within Greater London). Gatwick and Luton airports only offered domestic and very short haul flights; and only catered mainly for persons with local points of origins or destination and others outside of London for whom those two airports were easier to travel to then what would become known as London Heathrow Airport.

The airport has been known as London Heathrow Airport since January 1972, due to the developments of London Gatwick and Luton Airports

Chapter 16
Air Traffic Control Towers at London Heathrow Airport

The airport has had a number of Air Traffic Control Towers over its history.

Air Traffic Control Towers (As such) were not used anywhere until after the First World War.

The first control tower was constructed in 1930 on the northerly perimeter of the Great Western Aerodrome (As it was then known) when it was opened (nb The aerodrome was only available for private aircrafts).

The Government constructed another control tower further eastwards again on the northerly perimeter, when it started expanding the aerodrome for military aviation between 1940 and 1944. This tower remained operational until the tower in the central area was opened during December 1955.

The Government constructed the third control tower as an integral part of the Central Area; which was opened with the Central Area in December 1955.

When Terminal Five was constructed, it became necessary to build a new taller control tower as the existing one did not have "communication" access to this terminal – As the airport had to remain fully open at all times, the tower had to be constructed off the premises and then taken to its location on three trailers and erected its location overnight (The five hours when the airport is closed).

Chapter 17
Rivers Around London Heathrow Airport

17.1   The River Thames

It can be said that the River Thames forms a large semi – circle round London Heathrow Airport. In fact had the river been in a straight line to Windsor to anywhere west of Windsor, it would have passed the airport on the northerly side.

17.2   The River Colne

The source of the River Colne is in Hertfordshire and it flows into the River Thames in the centre of Staines. Once south of Hertfordshire, it forms the boundaries between Greater London (The county of Middlesex until April 1965) and Buckinghamshire and then between Berkshire and Surrey.

17.3   The River Crane

The source of the River Crane is to the south of Hayes, it passes London Heathrow Airport on the easterly side, it passes through Hounslow Heath on the westerly side, it passes through Twickenham and it flows into the River Thames between Kew and Richmond.

17.4   The Duke of Northumberland River and the Longford River

Both the Duke of Northumberland and the Longford rivers leave the River Colne north west of the airport and run in a south easterly direction. The Duke of Northumberland River runs to the east of Longford and to the north of Feltham where it joins the River Crane. The Longford River runs to the west of Longford and through Feltham to join the Thames near Hampton Court.

17.4.1 Their natural (Pre 1939) routes – The rivers respectively passed either side of the Perry Oaks Sludge Disposal Sewerage Works after these were brought into operation. South of the sewerage works:-

  a. The Duke of Northumberland River ran south eastwards virtually directly to East Bedfont.

b. The Longford River ran due south for three quarters of a mile and then due east to East Bedford (Determining the northerly boundaries of Stanwell and West Bedfont)

17.4.2 The position during the 1939 to 1945 Second World War – Between 1940 and 1944, the Government had both of these rivers re – routed in order to expand the two runways westwards:-

a. The Duke of Northumberland River – From the northerly perimeter of the runway, it was re – routed to the westerly and southerly perimeter of the runway to East Bedfont; round the Perry Oaks Sludge Disposal Sewerage Works to include the former natural route along the easterly boundary of these sewerage works.

b. The Longford River – Remain inside the perimeter road passing to the west of the Perry Oaks Sludge Disposal Sewerage Works next to the Stanwell Moor Road and then past the southerly runway and then due east between the Stanwell Moor Road and East Bedfont.(nb The rivers ran next to and parallel to each other between the south west of the sewerage works and East Bedfont)

17.4.3 The effects of Terminal Five – When Terminal Five was constructed between 2000 and 2008, both of these rivers were rerouted to remain outside of the perimeter road north, west and south west of the airport.

Chapter 18
Perry Oaks Village, Farm. And The Perry Oaks Sludge Disposal Sewerage Works

It is a good idea to consider the effects of London Heathrow Airport on Perry Oaks Village and the Perry Oaks Sludge Sewerage Works.

Perry Oaks was a village with a farm located in the then county of Middlesex immediately to the south of Longford, east of the Longford River and west of the Duke of Northumberland River. To the immediate west of the village was Tithe Barn Lane, which roughly followed a north/south route between Longford and Stanwell.

Neither the village, the farm, or Tithe Barn Lane were affected by the construction of the aerodrome between 1914 and 1918, nor by the aerodrome's use for private aircraft between 1930 and 1939; as the aerodrome (As it was then) was located some distance to the east.

The sludge disposal sewerage works were inaugurated in the early 1930s by the Middlesex County Council as a part of the West Middlesex Drainage Scheme as a result of the increase in population to the west of Middlesex subsequent to World War One. Beforehand were a total of twenty eight distinct small sewerage works inefficiently operated by different borough, rural and urban district councils.

The West Middlesex Drainage Scheme involved a large sewerage works at Mogden, Isleworth, the sludge disposal works at Perry Oaks and seventy miles of new pipes. Two million people were served within an area of 160 square miles. The main works in Mogden were in the middle of a populated area which would not tolerate a sludge works as a neighbour. The sludge was therefore pumped from Mogden to the disposal works to the west of Perry Oaks Village on the other (Westerly) side of Tithe Barn Lane; what was then a remote area some seven miles away from the main works at Mogden, where the settling lagoons would cause less of a problem. The site for the sludge works was chosen as it was then isolated from existing dwelling houses (Separated from Perry Oaks village and farm by Tithe Bam Lane), building development was then unlikely in the immediate vicinity, the land was low cost and it was three miles from the nearest train station.

The site of the sludge disposal works occupied 250 acres of land. The pipe from Mogden followed the route of the Bath Road and Tithe Barn Lane (nb Had the pipe taken a more direct route the construction of the airport to its present size would probably have been very difficult). The dried sludge was removed by road and then spread as a fertiliser on agricultural land. They were not a visual intrusion on the general landscape, from the air or from a distance they looked like open land (Grassland interspersed with water and scrub) and the area attracted birds.

Entry to the sludge disposal works was originally on the easterly side from Tithe Barn Lane (The village and farm were east of this lane).

Perry Oaks was one of the villages and farms which were destroyed between 1940 and 1944 to extend the runways westwards. Both the Longford and Duke of Northumberland Rivers were re – routed along the aerodrome's new perimeter road

The sludge disposal sewerage works themselves were not affected by the aerodrome's expansion as they were considered essential for health and safety reasons and there was nowhere else considered suitable for where to re – locate them. The Air Ministry revised its layout plans for the airport so as to avoid taking these.

A new road, the Stanwell Moor Road, was constructed between the A30 London Road and Bath Road (The route of the A4 until1925) in 1944, which passed to the immediate west of the sludge disposal sewerage works.

The entrance from Tithe Barn Lane was closed in 1944 as a result of the airport extension, since when entrance has been from the newly constructed Stanwell Moor Road.

The Thames Water Board took control of the sludge disposal sewerage works when control of water was nationalised and the sewage works have been controlled by Thames Utilities Plc since the privatisation of water.

These works had to be re – located between 2002 and 2005 as a result of the construction of Terminal Five. By this time newer forms of technology meant that the works only required a site 10% size of the original site. The transfer was to a site next to Iver Sewerage Works to the south of the M4 and North West of the original site. The name Iver is misleading due to the distance of the sludge disposal sewerage works from Iver in Buckinghamshire. The sewerage works are closer to Colnbrook.

The sewerage works remained intact and fully operational.

Chapter 19
The Public Observatory

The airport had become a magnate for people wanting to see aircrafts landing and taking off by 1949. People watched aircrafts land and take off from any place from which they could. A few people committed acts of trespass.

An observatory was therefore constructed.

By 1953, the airport's public observatory had become the most popular London activity with 527,000 visitors in that year alone; to include individual people, families, groups of children and school groups. It was known for twelve to sixteen year old school children to spend eight hours in the observatory. It was generally regarded as "a real novelty".

A new Observatory was relocated on the roof of the Queens Building and extended over the Europa and Britannic Buildings (As they were then known, Terminals One and Two as they became known in 1974) when these opened in December 1955 – There were commentaries of aircrafts landing and taking off – There were children's playgrounds with paddling pools, souvenir shops, easy chairs, covers in case it rained, coffee shops, restaurants, while many people brought their own hampers along – Coach parties could also be given a guided tour of the airport – Men wore suites and ties, ladies were well dressed and children wore their school uniforms to visit the observatory. On average, one million people visited these facilities each year between 1956 and 1971.

The Observatory was closed towards the end of 1971 because of the activities of the Irish Republican Army (I.R.A.); as it was basically the perfect place for a terrorist to make an attack on an aircraft. Also the Europa Building was to be demolished and when re – built (Then known as Terminal One) no provision was made for an observatory on top Terminal One (As then known) as no longer considered to be appropriate for security reasons.

The airport observatory was re – opened in 1978. However, it only attracted a few thousand visitors in each year and it was no longer a novelty. Passenger piers and building extensions obscured the views. It was only on the roofs of Terminal Two (As it had become known) and the Queens Building only. Also Terminal Three was on the opposite side of the Central area. As aviation was becoming within the financial means of more and more ordinary people, visiting airport the observatory was no longer a novelty.

The observatory was permanently closed to the public in September 2001.

Chapter 20
The London Administrative Area

The General Position Prior To 1888

Officially London was only the City of London and anywhere outside of that square mile was not in London. London (in essence the City of London) was inside the County of Middlesex. Westminster was a completely separate city; and elsewhere within present day Greater London, a mix of boroughs, urban, and rural districts.

There were six counties; three to the north of the Thames, namely Essex, Middlesex, and Buckinghamshire; and three to the south, namely Kent, Surrey, and Berkshire; with the Thames being a county boundary to as far as the Oxfordshire boundary. On the northerly side, the River Lea was the county boundary between Essex and Middlesex, and the River Colne the county boundary between Middlesex and Buckinghamshire. On the southerly side, the present day boundary between Southwark and Lambeth was the county boundary between Kent and Surrey, and the Great South West Road the county boundary between Surrey and Berkshire to as far as the Hampshire boundary. (nb The Great South West Road was the pre 1925 route of what, between 1925 and 1930, was re-routed and became known as the A30)

The boundary of the County of Middlesex was the northerly shore of the River Thames between the River Lea and the River Colne, the River Colne between the Thames and the Hertfordshire boundary, what is now the present day Greater London/Hertfordshire boundary between the River Colne and the River Lea, and the River Lea between the Hertfordshire boundary and the Thames.

The whole of the are which in due course would be a part of London Heathrow Airport consisted of a number of rural districts and parishes within the County of Middlesex. The idea that this are or its surroundings might be developed was "well over the horizon" at the time.

The Position In 1887

By 1888, the London conurbation had gradually expanded in size to what, since 1965, has been known as Inner London (The London County Council area between 1888 and April 1965). Various activities within this area had become controlled by joint boards or authorities, whether local authority, central government, public corporation, or otherwise controlled.

By 1888 outside the area as detailed in the previous paragraph, many built up communities had become larger and joined together, to include ones either side of the then county boundaries. This could be noticed along the Thames between Central London and the Oxfordshire boundary, the Great South West Road to as far as the Hampshire boundary, the River Colne to as far as the Hertfordshire boundary, and the River Lea to as far as the Hertfordshire boundary. Examples include Kingston, Maidenhead, and Reading on the Thames; Uxbridge on the Colne; Camberley on the Great South West Road. What has since become known as Staines was in four different counties; depending upon what side of the Thames, Colne and Great South West a particular locality was on.

The 1888 Local Government Act

The 1888 Local Government Act created the administrative County of London which was to be governed by its London County Council. The area within this administrative corresponded with the area known today as Inner London. It then consisted of the City of London, the City of Westminster, and a number of Metropolitan Boroughs.

The other change under the 1888 Local Government Act was that a number of changes were made to local authority boundaries outside of the 1888 to 1965 County of London, basically to ensure that all built up areas (as in 1888) were each in the same administrative county:-

East of the London County Council administrative area, the River Thames remained a county boundary.

West of the London County Council area the Thames and all built up areas which extended either side of it were in Surrey to as far as the west of Staines, and thereafter in Berkshire to as far as the Oxfordshire boundary.

North east of the County of London, the River Lea and all built up areas which extended either side of it were in Middlesex.

To the west of London, the River Colne was in Surrey until outside of the Staines built up area, and then with all built up areas which extended either side in Middlesex to as far as the Hertfordshire boundary.

To the south west of London, the Great South West Road and all built up areas which extended either side of it were in Surrey to as far as the Hampshire boundary.

The Area Around What Was To Become London Heathrow Airport 1920 To 1952

Until the early 1920's this consisted of a number of rural districts in the west of the County of Middlesex. There had been aerodromes on the site since 1915, and it was during the Second World War that the airport was developed to its current size. There was substantial development around the area between 1920 and 1952 as populations expanded and increased, and many rural districts were given urban district or borough status. The Perry Oaks Sludge Disposal Sewerage Works were inaugurated in the early 1930's by the Middlesex County Council as part of the West Middlesex Drainage Scheme due to the increase in population on the westerly side of Middlesex (these were located where Terminal Five has been since 2008, and could then be relocated as technology had enabled a much smaller site for the sludge disposal works).

Post 1965 Greater London

The administrative area of Greater London in its present form was created in April 1965 under the terms of the Local Government Act of 1965. This change was made as London conurbation had expanded considerably between 1920 and 1952, thought it has not expanded since 1952 because of green belt rules. Under the 1965 change, Greater London included most, but not all, of the London conurbation. It was not until then that the airport was within what could be described as the London administrative area (before then it was in what was then the County of Middlesex). The airport was then and remains in the London Borough of Hillingdon.

Summary Regarding the History of the Local Authority Administration of the Area of the Site Covered By London Heathrow Airport

In 1884, the whole of the area of the site which in due course would be a part of London Heathrow Airport was within a number of rural districts and parishes on the westerly side of the County of Middlesex. The idea that this area or its surroundings might be developed was "well over the horizon" at that time (as with any form of aviation other than balloons, kites, and birds).

There was substantial development around the area of the site between 1920 and 1952 as populations expanded and increased (in particular on the north easterly, easterly, south easterly, and southerly sides), and many of the rural districts around were given urban district or borough status.

The fact that the airport fell within a number of local authority administrations with differing statues and political leanings between when it was expanded to its current size in 1944 and the formation of Greater London in 1965 was not a problem, as the airport was expanded under wartime military regulations, and then belonged to the Crown until 1972.

It was in April 1965 under the terms of the Local Government Act of 1965 that it could be said that the whole of the airport as it has been since 1944 has been inside what could be described as the administrative area of London (i.e. Greater London) in an area covered by one single local administration (i.e. The London Borough of Hillingdon).

Chapter 21
The Airport Never Sleeps

What I mean by my statement The Airport Never Sleeps is much activity goes on within the airport twenty four hours of the day, even when it is generally closed to the public and there are no scheduled flight landings or take offs, and in fact there is activity which can only take place where there are no flights landing or taking off or passengers around - Unlike most bus, coach, and railway stations, and many smaller airports and seaports.

Security must be maintained throughout the premises at all times. Also security equipment can best be serviced at times that there are no flights or passengers.

On the airside:-

1. Runways have to be inspected, maintained, and repairs made. A small crack or pot hole in the concrete could cause very serious problems.

2. The lights around and the painted markings on the runways must be properly maintained; as pilots rely fully on these when taking off and landing. A missing light, a gap in the marking, inaccurate or unclear markings could create serious confusion for pilots. After all, pilots do use these to guide them when landing and taking off.

3. The grass beside and around runways must remain cut to the correct length.

4. The control tower and its equipment must be serviced and maintained to ensure that it is in full working order at all times that there are flights landing or taking off.

5. As far as aviation fuel is concerned, there must be a sufficient supply from before flights take off in any one day, supplies which must be maintained throughout the day. Also the pipes for the movement of this fuel and the equipment for fuelling aircrafts must be maintained and be in proper working order. A fault in the equipment could cause severe chaos as more and more flights could encounter lengthy delays through having to wait for fuel.

It is only overnight when no passengers are around that within passenger tenninals:-

1. Catering and retail outlets can be serviced with their food supplies and goods.

2. Lavatories and washing facilities can be serviced, cleansed, maintained, and when

necessary repaired.

3. The buildings themselves and all facilities within can be cleaned, maintained and when necessary repairs made.

4. The equipment for the movement of luggage between passengers and aircraft holds must remain in working order. As departing passengers check in and deposit their luggage, the luggage must be transported to the correct aircraft promptly and effectively. As arriving aircrafts land, all luggage must be transported to the baggage collection area as promptly as possible to the correct stands.

5. Cargo is transported to the Cargo Terminal throughout the day and night. It is out of necessity that a substantial amount of cargo must be transported from it original point of origin or taken to its final destinations overnight.

The public roads and other infrastructure for the public to gain access to and be able to leave the airport must be services, maintained, and when necessary repaired; to-gether with all of the service roads.

In fact the land sides of all of the terminals remain open overnight with at least one catering outlet. (The outlet generally only serves te coffee, hot chocolate, and soft drinks). There are passengers with flights scheduled to depart very early in the morning or to arrive late at night, who need to leave their points of origin before public transport opens or who could not reach their final destinations before public transport closes, and who therefore sleep on benches or on the floor with or without blankets. There are others who prefer to sleep on a terminal bench or on the floor as opposed to a late night land journey upon arrival or a virtual overnight journey to the airport.

Not permitted but does frequently take place is homeless people using the terminals for overnight shelter, somewhere indoors to stay, and inexpensive refreshments. Although they are ejected if it is realised that they are homeless people, no action is taken if they are able to look like tourists who have arrived on one of the last evening flights when there is no public transport to their fmal destination, or taking one of the first morning flights for which they cannot travel by public transport at the time of day from their point of origin. Likewise no action is taken during the day if they are tn the departure check in area and look as if they are waiting for friends or relatives, or inthe arrival area waiting for friends or relatives off flights.

Chapter 22
The Future of London Heathrow Airport (Post 2018)

No one can say with any degree of certainty what will happen to the airport and how it will develop in the future. One can only say for certain what has happened to-date, consider and think about ideas and suggestions as they are put forward.

Unlike airlines which can change relatively quickly in response to changing circumstances and demands, airports have to make long term planning decisions, sometimes as far as fifty years into the future. In fact Heathrow Airport itself developed from somewhat humble beginnings with no plans for it to take on any particularly significant role in aviation; to become the principal airport for the United Kingdom and one of the world's busiest airports.

Airports have to adapt to changes in aircraft designs and sizes.

There have to be two basis forms of investment:-
1. Infrastructure to include improved terminals, facilities and access to the airport.
2. Capacity to allow the maximum number of aircraft, passenger and cargo movements.

From time to time, suggestions have been made and ideas put forward, which have not been proceeded with for one or more reasons to include practicality, financial, viability and/or could cause more problems than they will solve. Other ideas have been "put on ice" due to other priorities, or they could cause problems or inconvenience for some affected people.

Terminal One is at present being re – built under a scheme similar to Terminal Five and the new Terminal Two and is due to re – ope1;1 around 2020. In a number aspects it will look as if Terminals One and Two will be a single terminal.

A Personal Rapid Transport System similar to that for Terminal Five (Which links that terminal to the business car park on the northerly perimeter and opened in April 2011), had been proposed for the Central

Area in 2014 but has been deferred due to practicalities and other priorities.

A baggage tunnel between the Central Area and Terminal Five is under consideration to make the movement of the luggage of passengers in transit who need to make such terminal changes easier.

Consideration has been given to the railway network continuing westwards from Terminal Five to link up with the national railway network to give access to:-

1. Reading via Egham, Virginia Water, Ascot and Wokingham.
2. Guildford via Egham, Virginia Water, Chertsey and Woking.
3. London Waterloo via Staines, Richmond and Clapham Junction.
4. Windsor

On 20th January 2009, support was given to the construction of a third runway and sixth terminal to the north, north west, or south west of the airport; but consideration of this was postponed in June 2010 due to opposition for various reasons. Other projects under consideration subsequent to 2010 but with no certainty regarding what further consideration will be given and their chances of proceeding have included:-

1. .A new airport in the Thames Estuary.
2. New runways and terminals at Gatwick, Luton and/or Stanstead Airport.
3. A new runway to the west of London Heathrow Airport with bridges over the M25, perimeter road and Stanwell Moor Road to link the runway and the necessary taxiways to the remainder of the airport.

The 2020, Covid 19 epidemic has had a very serious impact on the aviation industry throughout the world with all passenger airports and airlines adversely affected. The numbers of flying passengers have fallen to 15% of that in 2019, a significant number of flights have been cancelled, and a substantial number of redundancies both at airports and on airline. No one can say what the long term impact on the aviation industry will be.

Final Comment – British Airways and Its History

One cannot really write about London Heathrow Airport without giving some consideration to the United Kingdom's principal airline carrier, British Airways as it is knows in 2018 and has been known since 1972.

It must be noted that British Airways and the enterprises which were or were a part of British Airways have used all of the United Kingdom's main airports since formation and not just London Heathrow Airport.

In the early 1920s, the British government wanted there to be a large airline company to represent the British Empire (As it was then known). Imperial Airways Ltd was formed on 1st April 1924 by amalgamations between a number of aviation enterprises to operate services between London and all current/former members of the British Empire as then known (Including the United States of America as it was a part of the United Kingdom prior to the American War of Independence, Ireland and other locations within the United Kingdom).

In the 1930s the British government also wanted there to be a large airline company to represent British aviation throughout the European continent. The government was also concerned that Imperial Airways was concentrating on routes between the United Kingdom and locations outside of the United Kingdom, as opposed to domestic routes. British Airways Ltd was therefore formed on 1st January 1936 by amalgamations between a number of aviation enterprises operating within the United Kingdom and between the United Kingdom and the remainder of Europe.

Both of these companies used Croydon Airport between their formations and the Second World War.

At the outbreak of the Second World War in September 1939, all civil aviation ceased under the provisions of the Air Navigation Order 1939, all aircrafts were requisitioned by the Air Ministry (As it was known at the time) and were only available for military use. The war ended in 1945 and the Government transferred all aircrafts not required for military use over to civilian use on 1st January 1946.

On 4th February 1946, the British government:-

1. Nationalised both Imperial Airways Pic and British Airways.
2. Created a new public corporation, British South American Airlines, out of a number of smaller companies, to operate services between the United Kingdom and the southern half of the American continent. There remained numerous privately owned British based airline companies but these were short haul and did not use the larger airports generally.

All three of these nationalised airlines have mainly used London Heathrow Airport since 1946; but have also used other airports around the country for limited numbers of their services since then

The government decided to streamline its airline operations and avoid duplication between its three public corporations. The Airways Corporation Act was therefore passed in 1949 under which:-

1. Imperial Airways Ltd and British South American Airlines Ltd were amalgamated into a single public corporation, known as the British Overseas Airways Corporation (B.O.A.C.).
2. British Airways was renamed British European Airways (B.E.A.) to reflect the routes over which it operated.

The British Overseas Airways Corporation and the British European Airways respectively introduced Tourist Class accommodation on to their airlines on 21st November 1952 and 1st May 1958 respectively as with other airline operators within the United Kingdom and throughout the world (See the second to last paragraph on page four) and extended this facility to all their airlines over eighteen month periods respectively.

By December 1960, the British Overseas Airways Corporation was operating to/from all locations outside of Europe except for the Iron Curtain countries.

Also by December 1960, British European Airways was operating to/from the whole of Europe, the Mediterranean coast and North Africa except for the Iron Curtain countries. It was also operating services within the United Kingdom between London, Aberdeen, Birmingham, Edinburgh, Glasgow, Guernsey, the Hebrides, Inverness, Jersey, the Orkney and Shetland Islands.

The two corporations became a single corporation, British Airways, in January 1972 to combine their strengths and to be able to interchange aircrafts. At the same time, two other airline operators were also absorbed into this corporation, to include Cambrian Airlines (Which had operated

148

around South Wales) and Northeast Airlines (Which had operated around the north east of England.

As with other airlines around the world; "In House" entertainment was introduced to long haul First Class in 1972 and had been made available on all long haul accommodation by 1980; airline lounges for first class passengers were introduced in 1972, business class was introduced to all international flights between 1980 and 1982 and in fact replaced first class on all except for long haul flights; and subsequently the way in which it operated its various classes of travel and facilities.

In the late 1970s British Airways began to lose its monopoly over international travel as private operators started to enter into this market.

British Airways was privatised in February 1987.

First and business class passengers have also had access to airline lounges on the Land Side of the Arrival areas since 1995.

British Midland Airways Pic (Known as British Midland International or BMI since 2001) was taken over by British Airways Plc. This decision to make and accept the "take over" was made in December 2011, the deal was completed on 20th April 2012 and the merger had been fully implemented by 27th October 2012.

British Airways (As known in 2018 and since 1972) has used London Heathrow Airport and its terminals in the same way as other airline operators:-

1. It used terminal three for all long haul flights from January 1972 as with all other airlines and operated all domestic flights as with all other airlines and short haul international flights from terminal one from April 1974.

2. When terminal four opened in April 1986, it transferred all of its long haul flights from terminal three to this terminal, but kept all other flights in terminal one.

3. In April 1998, British Airways transferred some of its long haul operations to Terminal One and some of its European operations to Terminal Four in order to balance out its use of both terminals equally throughout the day; but kept all of its domestic services in Terminal One as the only terminal with a domestic section.

4. When Terminal Five opened in March 2008, British Airways transferred all of its services to this terminal; whether domestic, European, or long haul (nb This terminal has only been used by British Airways).

5. Its takeover of British Midland International (BMI) in 2012, meant its return to Terminal One as it took over that company's domestic and short haul international slots in there.

6. In order that all flights to and from each location always used the same terminal, a number of domestic and short haul international routes were switched between terminals one and five.
7. When Terminal One closed in June 2015 for demolition and re – building, British Airways was allocated slots in Terminal Three. To be in line with other airline operators, it was then decided that a mix of both short and long haul routes would use Terminal Three.

A typical long haul British Airways flight accommodates 401 passengers, of which fourteen passengers are seated in first class, twenty eight in business class, fifty five in premium economy and the remaining 304 in economy.

Between 2013 and 2018, British Airways:-
1. .Employed 40,000 people worldwide in seventy five countries but mainly in the United Kingdom; to include 15,000 cabin crew, 3,500 pilots and 3,800 in headquarters.
2. Had 270 aircrafts (50% long haul) 220 of which were based in the United Kingdom.
3. There were 300 000 flights in each year.
4. Purchases have been anything between a new aircraft and sausages for meals.
5. British Airways aircrafts have taken off somewhere in the world every seventy five seconds.
6. At any one time there have been at least 5,000 members of cabin crew on duty.

Crew planning and efficient crew rostering are essential to ensure that the correct numbers of crew members are available at all locations as required (Whether within the airport or abroad).

British Airways has large dedicated staff training facilities

While aircrafts are in the air, the company at ground level remains in constant radio contact with their crews.

British Airways has its own operations centre in Terminal Five as the terminal is dedicated to British Airways.

Some Statistics

Cargo and mail in tons – Total distances in miles.

	Distances	Passengers	Cargo	Mail
Imperial Airways				
1924/5	853,042	11,395	391,032	N/A
1930/1	1,295,848	20,993	1,017,773	N/A
1937/8	6,223,968	62,105	8,353,618	N/A
British Overseas Airways Corporation				
1946/7	23,185,787	129,928	1,677,000	1,795
1947/8	25,470,631	115,675	2,447,000	2,088
1950/1	27,767,173	196,512	5,598,000	2,272
1995/6	36,039,591	371,215	7,979,000	3,815
1960/1	64,948,897	785,082	12,921,000	5,548
British European Airways				
1946/7	3,135,000	71,177	668,000	510
1947/8	12,337,000	551,522	2,610,000	1,558
1950/1	20,586,000	939,586	10,079,000	5,249
1955/6	26,895,000	2,224,747	18,500,000	7,895
1960/1	40,150,667	3,990,957	41,996,000	8,850
Qantas Empire Airways				
1935/6	600,000	2,074	22,000	42
1937/8	1,000,000	2,913	66,000	80
1946/7	5,800,000	26,764	587,000	355
1947/8	6,300,000	31,048	1,170,000	318
1950/1	9,700,000	85,000	8,000,000	850
1955/6	13,000,000	150,000	10,000,000	1,400
1960	16,140,000	193,876	27,404,881	1,746

Developments in Airline Fares Throughout History

Fares have fallen over the years, in real terms though not necessarily in monetary terms. 1965 first class fares we 70% of the 1953 fares in real terms when there was only one class, with 1965 tourist class fares 60% of the then first class fares. 2015 first class fares on long haul flights and business class fares on short haul flights were between 50% and 80% of the 1965 first class fares in real terms. 2015 standard class fares could be as low as 10% of the first class fares with one or two interim classes on long haul flights. Post 1978 "Low Cost No Frills" airlines have offered even less expensive flights.